K9 SCHUTZHUND TRAINING

Become a better trainer with the K9 Professional Training Series

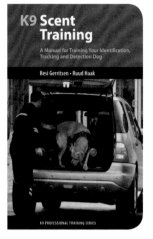

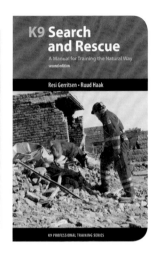

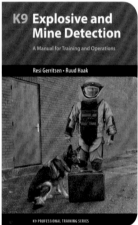

The K9 Professional Training Series teaches proven, effective, and positive training methods from highly experienced and respected trainers from Europe and North America. These uniquely authoritative manuals combine expert knowledge with detailed graphics and images.

See the complete list at

dogtrainingpress.com

K9 SCHUTZHUND TRAINING

A Manual for IGP Training through Positive Reinforcement

Updated second edition

Dr. Resi Gerritsen
Ruud Haak

K9 Professional Training series

An imprint of
Brush Education Inc.

Brush Education Inc.
www.brusheducation.ca
contact@brusheducation.ca

Editorial: Meaghan Craven
Cover: John Luckhurst; Cover image: Marcel Jancovic/Shutterstock 79465981
Interior design: Carol Dragich, Dragich Design
Interior images: Ruud Haak: pages 6, 33, 37, 38 up, 50, 66, 67, 68, 72, 79, 87 both, 107, 129, 170, 177, 184, 205, and 240. Markus Mohr: pages 5, 11, 26, 28, 29, 38 down, 42 both, 45, 47 both, 52, 56, 58, 60, 77, 81, 82, 83, 89, 90, 94, 99, 101, 102 all three, 113, 118, 120, 122, 123, 126, 131, 141, 144, 147, 152, 159, 160, 165, 168, 172, 183, 197 both, 206, 209 both, 213, 215, 216 both, 217 both, 218, 228, 232, 234, 235, 239, and 241.
Illustrations: Chao Yu, Vancouver

Printed and manufactured in Canada

Library and Archives Canada Cataloguing in Publication
Title: K9 schutzhund training : a manual for IGP training through positive reinforcement / Dr. Resi Gerritsen, Ruud Haak.

Other titles: Canine schutzhund training

Names: Gerritsen, Resi, author. | Haak, Ruud, 1947- author.

Description: Updated second edition. | Series statement: K9 professional training series | Includes bibliographical references.
Identifiers: Canadiana (print) 20200348140 | Canadiana (ebook) 20200348647 | ISBN 9781550598711 (softcover) | ISBN 9781550598728 (PDF) | ISBN 9781550598735 (Kindle) | ISBN 9781550598742 (EPUB)

Subjects: LCSH: Schutzhund dogs—Training. | LCSH: Schutzhund (Dog sport
Classification: LCC SF428.78 .G47 2021 | DDC 636.7/0886—dc2

Contents

Phase C   Protection

Preface

Since 2000, when the first edition of *K9 Schutzhund* was published, the methods for training dogs—including Schutzhund training—have changed. Today, positive reinforcement is the accepted method. With this in mind, we have rewritten *K9 Schutzhund* to help you train your dog for IGP (Internationale Gebrauchshunde Prüfungsordnung; formerly called IPO or Schutzhund) levels 1, 2, and 3, employing the newest methods based on classic and operant conditioning. The methods we recommend for teaching your dog tracking, obedience, and protection exercises are all supported by the excellent results dog trainers have seen when they use positive reinforcement.

More than ever before, handlers need a clear and well-organized manual to help them train dogs to undergo IGP trials. That is why we, with our years of experience as professional dog trainers and instructors, went to work on designing a practical training method. Of course, writing about K9 training is not easy. For example, some old-fashioned training methods are still in use, and the heated discussions that arise between proponents of new and old methods sometimes muddied the waters as we set out to write this book about modern IGP training.

We persisted, however, and our research (based on practice) has proven that the new methods described here are very successful. We must emphasize that it is impossible to learn K9 training solely by reading this or any other book. To successfully train your dog, you must work with him on a training field under the direction of a professional instructor and helpers (skilled tracklayers and decoys). This book is only meant to provide theoretical support to the work done on the training field.

The new method described in this book does not provide a fast and easy way to train a dog. All training begins with a bond between handler and dog. If that bond is lacking, the handler will find it impossible to work with the animal. Handler and dog must understand and know each other completely, which is only possible when they spent a lot of time together. The handler must first and foremost love his dog; the dog should never be seen as merely an object to train or work.

When the handler and dog have established a good relationship and communication, it is possible to teach the dog what is required in certain exercises. Some dogs learn quickly, but others need more time. The amount of time needed to train a dog depends not only on its breed but also on its individual personality and needs. Handlers must be patient.

Dogs learn best when training is conducted in a low drive, or when they are not agitated or excited. When in a low drive, dogs can focus on behaving properly and listening to the dog handler's encouragement and commands. For some dogs, such as those that are easily excited, learning in a high-motivation or -drive environment is difficult because they become hysterical and cannot understand what is expected of them. They are aware of everything going on around them and, as a result, will be active without knowing what they are doing, displaying behavior that is inappropriate for the situation. So, take your time, provide the right, "low-drive" environment, and your patience will be rewarded.

Good K9 training takes months, even years, but the results will be solid. A dog trained too quickly always shows that he is performing under duress because of the high-pressure environment in which he trained. Building a good relationship with a dog, laying the foundation for a long and pleasant partnership, takes a lot of time. We cannot emphasize enough how important that relationship is; the combination of handler and dog will fail if the pair does not have a strong relationship.

Training, both as a hobby and as a profession, should be pleasant for the dog and the handler. It should be a successful learning process that yields progress for both parties. If training becomes a torment for the handler or the dog, then both parties are on the wrong track.

When training your dog, encourage him to use his natural characteristics, but don't exploit them! The harmonious agreement between you and your dog is the foundation for all activities, regardless of the sport the pair of you engage in. To achieve harmony, it is important to go into the dog's world and understand his abilities. In the end, only someone who is a true friend to his dog will take a healthy and capable dog to training, trials, and competitions.

If you have, after reading this book, a better understanding of K9 training and can complete a fine training period with your dog, with good results at the trials, we will have achieved the goal we had in mind when writing this book.

We wish to thank Mr. Markus Mohr from Austria (www.hstc.at or

www.facebook.com/HundeSportTrainingscenter) for all his advice and
for the excellent photographs he contributed to this book. He showed us
the enormous advantage of this modern way of training K9s in the IGP
Schutzhund program, and for that we are most grateful.

This updated second edition includes changes to the IGP program,
making this book a complete and up-to-date manual for the International Utility Dogs Regulations (IGP).

Changes to the Internationale Gebrauchshund Prüfung (IGP)

As of January 1, 2019, the Internationale Prüfungsordnung (IPO) was
renamed to Internationale Gebrauchshund Prüfung (IGP), and new
rules came into effect. The IGP Regulations can be found on the website
of the Fédération Cynologique Internationale (FCI). Following is a brief
overview of the most important changes:

TRACKING

• The IGP 1, 2, and 3 levels of tracking will all use 3 articles, each
worth 7 points for a total of 21 points for the articles.

OBEDIENCE

• In all IGP levels, the distance the handler has to throw the dumbbell
is more clearly defined as approximately 10 meters.
• The minimum distance from the hurdle or scaling wall is defined as
4 meters (no longer 5 paces).
• In IGP 1, there is no longer a "retrieve over the scaling wall" test.
Instead, dogs are assessed on their ability to "climb over the scaling
wall":
 – The dog handler takes the basic position in front of the scaling
 wall.
 – After giving the command to Sit, the handler goes to the other
 side of the wall and stands at a distance of at least 4 meters to
 the scaling wall.
 – On the judge's cue, the handler calls the dog with the commands
 for jumping and coming.
 – The dog must come with powerful climbing to his handler and
 sit straight and close in front.
 – After a 3 second pause, the handler gives the command for the
 dog to go into the final basic position.

- The evaluation criteria for the "send out with down" exercise are more clearly defined.

PROTECTION

- The IGP protection test still includes pressure and stick contact (soft stick hits) and an "attack on the dog in motion" (long bite / courage test) at all levels, with slight differences for levels 1 and 2. In countries where laws prohibit the stick test, these regulations can be implemented without it.
- IGP 1 no longer requires a blind search of the 5th blind. The dog will instead be sent directly into the 6th blind (final blind) for the exercise "search for the helper."
- In IGP 1, the handler is allowed to leash the dog during pickup and transport exercises.
- IGP 2 has no "attack on the dog in the back transport" exercise, but has an additional re-attack (defense against an attack in the guarding phase) exercise with no stick contact after the "attack on the dog in motion" (long bite / courage test), like the IGP 3.
- In IGP 1 and IGP 2, for the exercise "attack on the dog in motion" (long bite / courage test), the helper doesn't have to return to the blind and then run out to the mid-line and towards the dog/handler. Instead the helper will remain mid-field after the last defense exercise and the handler will pick up the dog and heel away down the mid-line of the field to a distance of approximately 30 meters away for the IGP 1 and 40 meters away for the IGP 2. Then the handler stops and turns towards the helper, where the judge will signal the exercise to begin.

Dr. Resi Gerritsen and Ruud Haak
January 2021

Disclaimer

While the contents of this book are based on substantial experience and expertise, working with dogs involves inherent risks, especially in danger-ous settings and situations. Anyone using approaches described in this book does so entirely at their own risk and both the author and publisher disclaim any liability for any injuries or other damage that may be sus-tained.

Introduction: The IGP Trials

According to the *International Utility Dogs Regulations* of the Fédération Cynologique Internationale (FCI), a dog can be trained and tested in the following trials:

- Preliminary Trial (IGP-V)
- International Utility Dog Trial 1 (IGP 1)
- International Utility Dog Trial 2 (IGP 2)
- International Utility Dog Trial 3 (IGP 3)

Each of these trials always has three phases:
- Phase A: Tracking
- Phase B: Obedience
- Phase C: Protection

The IGP trials serve two purposes. First, when dogs pass a trial, we know they are suitable for the job they are doing. Second, the trials help breeders maintain and improve certain qualities in their dogs from generation to generation. If a dog passes a trial, he or she is considered breed worthy. Furthermore, the trials contribute to the health and fitness of the deployed dogs, not to mention that of their handlers.

On the day of testing, the dog must meet the required age limit—no exceptions are permitted.

- IGP-V: 15 months
- IGP 1: 18 months
- IGP 2: 19 months
- IGP 3: 20 months

A dog handler may only participate in one trial per day and may show a maximum of two dogs at a given trial. A dog may only achieve one title at a trial. Verbal commands are single-word orders that should be spoken briefly and at a normal volume. The commands may be given in any language, but the same command must be used for the same exercise at all times; this is the case for all phases.

The dog handler has to carry a leash throughout the trial, either worn around the shoulders (clasp side away from the dog) or kept somewhere out of sight. In addition, during the trial, the dog must wear a simple, single-row, loose-fitting large link collar, which is not hooked to the live setting. The collar may not have spikes, claws, or other hooks. Other collars—leather, pinch, etcetera—are not permitted during a trial. The judge ensures that this is the case at all times. Flea or tick collars must also be removed prior to the trial.

The handler must present the dog in a sporting manner, and regardless of the results in any given phase, the handler is obliged to complete the remaining phases of the event.

Temperament Test

The judge will normally begin a trial by conducting a temperament test (also called an impartiality test) to find out whether or not the dog is uninhibited (i.e., trusting and gets along well with other people and dogs). Dogs that are not uninhibited cannot take part in the examination and will be disqualified. Some examples of inhibited behavior include when dogs cannot be approached, show timidity or aggression, and try to bite someone. The dog's behavior will also be assessed throughout the trial. The judge is obliged to disqualify any dog that displays a faulty temperament at any time during the trial. Another important part of the test is the identity inspection (checking the tattoo or the chip number). Dogs that do not pass this test may not participate in the trial.

The judge must perform the temperament tests under normal conditions in a location that is neutral for the dog. All participants present their dogs—on a loosely held leash—separately to the judge. Of course, the judge must avoid any provocation, but the dog must be comfortable with being touched if necessary.

The judge will assess dogs according to the following three criteria:

1. *Positive behavior*: The dog conducts herself in a neutral, self-confident, sure, attentive, energetic, and impartial manner.

2. *Still acceptable, but borderline cases*: The dog is slightly
   unstable, slightly nervous, or slightly insecure. This dog
   is still permitted to undergo the trial but is to be closely
   monitored for the duration.
3. *Negative behavior or faulty temperament*: The dog bites or is
   shy, insecure, scared, gun-shy, out of control, or aggressive.
   This dog must be disqualified.

Scoring

The evaluation of the dog's performance is noted with ratings (qualification) and points. Qualification and the corresponding points reflect the quality of the respective exercise, phase, and trial. The ratings for IGP 1, 2, and 3 are as follows:

Qualification	Percentage	Points per phase A, B, or C	Points per trial
Excellent	at least 96%	100–96	300–286
Very Good	95–90%	95.5–90	285–270
Good	89–80%	89.5–80	269–240
Satisfactory	79–70%	79.5–70	239–210
Insufficient	under 70%	69.5–0	209–0

The dog can be said to have "passed" a trial when she has received a minimum of 70 per cent of the possible points. The judge only awards full points during the evaluation of a particular phase. However, within individual exercises, partial points can be given. To come to a final result, the judge rounds partial points up or down. To succeed, the dog needs to receive at least 70 points per phase A, B, and C, and per trial at least 210 points.

Participating in the Trial

When you are absolutely sure that your dog is tracking well and performs all the obedience and protection exercises correctly, you may wish to participate in an IGP trial. Begin with IGP-V or IGP 1. Prepare yourself well for the trial and be aware of what will happen. Study the IGP trial regulations (*International Utility Dogs Regulations*) and find out what is allowed and what is not.

On the day of the trial, leave home early and make sure you are there on time. One is always a bit nervous on a trial day, and you can easily transmit that emotion to your dog. To help guard against exciting your dog, follow the routine you usually enact on a normal training day. Wear the same clothes you usually wear for training, leave home in the same way, and don't do or bring other things that are strange to you and your dog. Sticking with your routine will help your dog stay on an even keel as you set out for the trial.

Of course, before you can set out with your dog to your first IGP trial, you must embark together on a training journey. The following chapters, organized in sections that outline the three phases of IGP training (Tracking, Obedience, and Protection), will help guide you.

Phase A

Tracking

Tracking Basics

Dogs are olfactory animals; their sense of smell provides them with more information about their environment than any of their other senses, and so they will perceive through this sense before any other. When we observe wild, canine-related packs, we see the older animals teaching the young the basics of hunting and tracking enemies in their territory. Dogs and their relatives carry out hunting and tracking duties by relying on their sense of smell and hearing. A dog's hearing is a lot better than a human's, which is very primitively equipped. However, humans normally see better than dogs do, especially objects across great distances, which is partly because of our height relative to the dog's. Consider how low to the ground a dog is; try getting down at a dog's level and look for an object located at a distance, one that you could see when you were standing. It is no accident of evolution that the dog's sense of smell and auditory capacity is so much superior to that of humans. Combined, these senses allow dogs to maintain themselves in a world of danger. And their sense of smell has helped humans many times through history.

Even in this age of great technology, we still make grateful use of the dog's superior ability to smell. There are drug and explosive detector dogs, as well as avalanche dogs and search-and-rescue dogs deployed after earthquakes or other disasters. There is still no replacement for the wonderful nose of the dog. Before we talk about the track and tracking, we want to explain briefly how the dog's nose works.

The Dog's Nose Knows

The inside of the dog's nose is its olfactory area, a surface covered by mucous membrane and olfactory cells that are sensitive to the least amount of odorants present in the air. With the support of the nervous system, these cells send their information about smells to the brain.

The dog's nose is not only bigger than a human's but its structure is also more complicated, consisting of a great many folds. As well, the olfactory center in the dog's brain comprises a much larger percentage of the total brain than the related center in the human brain. To continue the comparison, the olfactory area inside the dog's nose is about 20 times thicker in dogs than in humans. A human has about 5 million olfactory cells, while the German shepherd has more than 200 million. The total size of the olfactory area in a human is 1.6–1.9 inches^2 (4–5 cm^2), while that of a German shepherd is about 67 inches^2 (170 cm^2). This means that the German shepherd has 34 times more olfactory area than a human. Thirty-four people on a tracking field can't smell what one dog can! Even compared to others in the animal world, dogs are in the forefront in terms of smelling power. That's nothing to sniff at.

For the dog, it is not unusual to interpret the world through the nose. From the day they are born, dogs must smell everything in their environment in order to get used to it. For example, the odor of the litter on a toy or piece of blanket that you bring home with your puppy is very important. That smell makes the puppy feel comfortable: a well-known smell among all the strange and new odors of its new home.

When your young dog walks around your house, it sniffs at everything, and while it does so will create memories of odors.

In doing so, the dog learns to discriminate between things (and between humans). It is a big mistake not to allow our dogs to smell everything. Maybe visitors to your home don't like to be sniffed, but for the dog, sniffing humans is necessary, just as it is necessary to sniff at other dogs or their droppings.

Dogs are always sniffing at each other's backsides because important sources of odor are located there. The sexual organs are, of course, very important, but the anal glands also emit telling odorants. The anal glands secrete a foul-smelling liquid, which is stored in the anal sacs. The odor of the liquid is characteristic to each animal; dogs have to sniff each other's backsides to find out who they are dealing with. When we don't allow dogs to get used to each other in this way, or don't give them the chance to sniff at the droppings of another dog because in our opinion it is "dirty," we deprive them of a lot of information. Let your dog pick up as many odors as possible; after all, he lives in a world of odors.

Always reward a young dog for intensively investigating odors. When tracking, we make good use of the dog's drive to smell. However, while smelling is something all healthy dogs can do very well, they must learn tracking. In Schutzhund training, we

In Schutzhund training, the dog must be able to follow a human track and locate articles that belong to the tracklayer placed at the track.

demand that the dog use its olfactory sense to follow a human track and locate articles that belong to the tracklayer.

The Track

When we walk through a meadow wet with morning dew, we leave behind a track where the grass is damaged and the dew is brushed off. If we were to leave and then come back after an hour, the track will have disappeared: the sun will have burned off the dew and most of the grass will have straightened up. That is, upon returning we would no longer be able to *see* the track. It would, however, still be there. In fact, for a reasonably experienced tracking dog with his nose to the ground, the track would not be difficult to work out.

When we walk over a dewy meadow, we are doing much more than creating a visible track. We also leave on the ground a bit of the odorant from our feet, which comes through our footwear. The smell of our shoes or boots and what is stuck to the soles stays behind on the track, too. Also, by walking over the grass, we damage it—how much depends on our weight, footwear, and the way we walk. We trample the grass flat, break plants, move leaves, and destroy twigs, and we compress the ground under our feet. As we walk, destruction in our wake, we disturb the normal odor of the ground: damaged leaves, plants, and grasses secrete a strong and penetrating odor. As well, the pressure of our feet on the ground warms it, marking our

If you create a track through morning dew, it's easy to see at first. After an hour, however, you'll need the dog's nose to find it!

temporary presence. All of these factors make where our feet fell smell different from where they didn't: these factors distinguish our track from everywhere else in the meadow.

The odors of the track dissolve slowly in the surrounding air, and the warmth we left behind will also disappear soon after the track is laid. The influences of temperature, wind, and humidity determine how long odors stay on the track. Under normal weather conditions (about 64°F [18°C], and little wind) the human odors in a meadow will slowly decrease after around two hours to less than half their strength after about eight hours. After about 12 hours, the odors will have greatly decreased and, in some cases, disappeared.

The odor of damaged plants and grasses stays, under normal weather conditions, at the same level for about eight hours. This is because of the powerful work of microbes on the damaged plants, an influence that compares to that of rotting bacteria. This smell of damaged plants—the bruised and broken plants and grasses—greatly influences the odor of a track.

When a dog is investigating a freshly laid track, it may search for a combination of human odor and damaged plants, but on older tracks, where only the odor of the damaged plants on the ground surface remains, that dog will have to employ other methods. A well-trained tracker dog knows that this special ground odor will keep him on the right track. Now and then a good tracker dog will smell beside the track, convincing himself of the location of the track as he senses the difference in smell between the two places. This movement to smell at the sides of the track will sometimes cause the dog to swing a bit, especially if the track has been blown away by the wind. You may at first think this swinging indicates poor tracking movement, but it's okay: a good tracker dog controls himself this way. Of course, that swinging should never become too extreme under normal weather conditions; if it does, you know that your dog is rummaging to find the track.

When laying a track for a dog to follow, it is important to walk normally through the field and not shuffle or kick down the ground. The odor does not become stronger on the ground when you kick it in, as some people might think. Rather, if kicked, the strong odor of the upper surface of the earth will come up. Shuffling over the ground also damages the surface of the soil. By laying a track using normal steps and a normal pace, we prevent the addition of too many superfluous and distracting ground odors to the total of the track odors. As well, we do the owner of the field a favor by not damaging the grounds.

When the dog comes to the track, he can tell the difference between fresh tracks and older ones. If this were not the case, a wild dog might track away from its prey instead of toward it. Under normal tracking conditions, a dog will walk from the older,

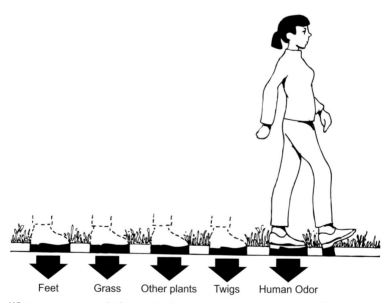

Feet   Grass   Other plants   Twigs   Human Odor

When you create a track, the weight of your body presses down on the soil, and grasses, plants, twigs, and insects are damaged, releasing odors particular to each. These smells, combined with those of bacteria and the smell of your feet—which comes through your shoes or boots and stays for a while on the ground—create an olfactory sensation for dogs.

weaker set of odors to the younger, fresher ones, and so it will walk the track in the right direction: from beginning to end.

The conditions of the terrain on which you lay a track influence how your dog investigates the track and works it out. For example, ploughed land or a grass-covered field, a bit moistened by morning dew, retains more odor than terrain with dry dirt or a sandy surface. Regardless of the terrain, it is important that the tracking field be fresh and that there were no people or animals present shortly before you lay your track. There are, however, some variables that you cannot completely control when laying the track. Weather is one of them.

Influence of the Weather

Wind speed and wind direction are important conditions to consider in tracking. When it is calm, the track you lay will last longer, and when your dog comes to such a track soon after it is laid, he will follow the track exactly as it was set down. However, even if the weather is calm, the strength of the track's odor will decrease over time. Still, how long a dog can work out the track after it was laid depends mostly on weather conditions. There are interesting stories about dogs working out old tracks from two days to a week old. The former, in our opinion, is more probable than the latter— but even the former timeframe is quite amazing and shows just how well the nose of a trained dog can work.

Truly calm weather is very rare, and even a light wind will move the track. When this happens, trainers say that the track is windblown. Of course, the direction the wind is blowing and the strength of the wind force determine how blown apart the track becomes. When windblown, a track's odor will be blown to the side. Thus, a dog following a windblown track will not always walk on the laid track but beside it, sometimes as much as half a yard off. How far the track is blown away by wind depends on when the track was laid and when the wind came up. On a windy day, a track created a short time, about twenty minutes, before you and your dog arrive to investigate it will not be blown away very far, but a track laid an hour or more before may already be blown away. Take the action of wind into account when observing your dog's actions on or near a track. For example, if a dog seems to be wandering aimlessly, an inexperienced handler may think the animal is taking a stroll through the tracking field instead of using his nose to search for the track.

Dogs that search too far away from a windblown track may at first, especially in the initial training phase, miss the articles lying on the track because they are passing them at too great a distance. But we should never mistrust the dog's nose. Articles heavily soaked in the odor of the tracklayer are not difficult for dogs to locate, even on a windblown track. When dogs pause in their efforts, keeping their nose a bit high for a while, and catch the scent of the article, they usually immediately locate the articles.

Windblown tracks happen all the time. Regardless, dogs that track with a "deep" nose—one positioned as close as possible to the ground's surface—will usually still search very close to the original footsteps of the track, where the odor remains strongest. When preparing for IGP tests, it is important to teach dogs to track with a deep nose. This can be done by making the conditions as ideal as possible, especially when you first begin training. Investigating a track in a field with short grass is a good place to start training because in long grass, the dog can see the track and it isn't necessary for him to use his nose. Another "easy" track to follow—and so one to avoid—is one whose odor is blowing toward the dog: a track set against the wind. With such tracks, dogs hardly have to put their noses to the ground in order to pick up the scent of the track, much less that of the articles they are to find. Training on easy tracks like these can encourage dogs to search with a high nose, not a deep one.

Obviously, the most advantageous weather conditions for tracking are those in which the early morning dew is disappearing

If you are training your dog to undergo IGP tests, make sure you teach him to track with a "deep nose," ensuring that his nose is as close as possible to the ground while he is tracking.

and there is little or no wind. Strong winds place the tracking dog at a disadvantage. However, if the dog is investigating a track with a slight wind coming from behind, he will be able to work out the track, but he will have to use a deep nose to do so.

The Start

Where the track begins is called the start. You should always be able to recognize the start so you know where your dog has to begin tracking. To indicate the start, place a marker, such as a stake, a colored dowel, a flag, or an iron rod. IGP regulations require that the stake is placed in the ground at your left side. The dog needs to pick up the odor of the track at the start, which is why you should intensively cover the ground surface there with your odor. There are two methods of teaching the dog to take to the track at the start: training with food or kibble, or training with a ball or toy. Choose your method with the temperament and drives of your dog in mind. Also, remember that it is best if dogs learn something new in a low drive. Only when your dog is in low drive will he be calm enough to survey the whole situation and learn.

The importance of low drive and training will be discussed more extensively in Phase B, the obedience part of this book.

If your dog has an average or low temperament, the ball/toy method will work well. Dogs with a high temperament, such as a Malinois, are better served by using the food/kibble method. For a dog that already has a high temperament, learning in a high drive with a ball or toy is very difficult. Instead of learning, they usually become hysterical.

Tracking with Food

This method, fully described in the chapter Tracking with Treats, is used by many handlers. When you use this method, slices of sausage, chunks of meat or cheese, dog biscuits, or dog food are used as incentives. Make sure you ration your dog's daily portion of food on training days so that he is motivated by the training food.

At first, don't lay a track but place small pieces of food at the start position. Your dog will learn to find those pieces and figure out what he has to do at the start, that is, take in the odor of the track, which begins at the start. Once the dog knows where the start is and what to do there, begin making short tracks, placing a piece of kibble or other food in every footstep. Through this, your dog learns that there is a close association between food and the tracklayer's footsteps, and he will begin tracking those footsteps intently, with his nose close to the ground.

When starting to train a new dog, you may wish to set up a short, straight track of about 10 to 20 paces, with a tail wind to prevent the dog searching with a high nose. Then, place a piece of food at the start. To entice your dog to move in the right direction, place a piece of food on the track every eight to 12 inches (20 to 30 cm). If your dog is searching well, increase the spacing of the food to about 16 inches (40 cm), then to 20 inches (50 cm), and finally to 39 inches (1 m). The first few times, you may wish to place a bit of extra bait, one piece after another, around the turns in the track.

THE DRAG TRACK

When you begin training a new dog, you may wish to create a super-smelly track by dragging meat over the ground. Normally such a drag track is laid by tying the meat to a rope or a line, or placing the meat in some hose. At the start, stand on the meat for several moments, ensuring the start has a strong meat odor. As you lay the track, try pushing the meat forward using one foot, which also creates a strong, meat-scented track. Try to lay this track with the wind at your back to prevent your dog from searching with a high nose. Finally, place a few pieces of meat at the end of the track as a reward.

During the first few training days, this drag track should be no longer than about 10 paces. Depending on your dog's interest level, you will work out between four and eight short tracks per training day. As soon as your dog demonstrates he is able to work out these tracks correctly, devise fewer but longer tracks to train on. Make the drag tracks successively longer until you can work out about a hundred paces of track without problems. After that, you can start creating tracks that have turns.

THE INTERRUPTED DRAG TRACK

Another common food/kibble method is the interrupted drag track. You, the handler, pack a piece of meat into a netting bag or some hose, which you then attach to a rope or leash and drag over the ground. Again, begin by creating a short, straight track with a tail wind. At the start, stamp the meat underfoot for a moment or two before dragging it for a few yards. After that, pick up the meat, touching it to the ground every second step; then, after some yards, every fourth step until the end of the track, where you should lay down some pieces of meat.

When your dog shows he is ready to progress from a short track to a long, straight track, and then on to a track with turns, make sure that you drag the meat along the ground around each turn. As soon as he is consistently successful on tracks with meat-scented turns, you can try just marking the start of the turns with meat, and then again after the turns. Your dog will progress to the point where he works out these tracks well, too, and at that point you can reduce the amount of meat-dragging along the whole track. Start by just touching the meat to the ground on every fifth step, later on every 10th step, and so on. Do not place any articles on the interrupted drag track in the beginning.

Tracking with a Ball or Toy

For this method, use a toy the dog likes to play with, such as a tennis ball or an old leather glove. Put the ball or toy in your pocket—where it will absorb your odor—for at least half an hour. Then, start beside the stake (which should be on your left) and walk forward about 13 feet (4 m) in a straight line, toward where you plan to lay the track. Make your steps short, with footprints overlapping each other (no spaces between), and keep your legs close together as you walk, so right and left footprints are close to each other as well. When you've walked the 13 feet (4 m) in this manner, stop and take a small step to the right. Your left foot should remain on the track you just made, and your right foot should be right beside it. Walk straight backward, slowly stepping so that your left foot stays on the earlier track, until you are back at the stake. (You could also turn so your right foot stays in

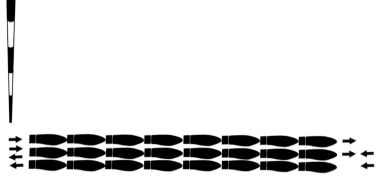

To make a good start for your dog, one that is covered with odor that will be easy for him to pick up, create a track that is three closely spaced footsteps wide.

the earlier track and your left foot makes a new track.) Stay there for about half a minute. In front of you, the track is partially laid: three shoes wide and the steps close together (no gaps) on all sides. Now, start laying the rest of the track. First, step forward using short paces along the middle of the earlier track; and after that you can step with normal paces. Position the toy or ball at the end of the track.

When you lay the track in this way, you ensure there is a lot of odor at the start, which your dog will pick up immediately. When he smells that the track is going past the start line, he will follow. While walking over the start, your dog has all the olfactory cues he needs to pick up the odor of the track.

When you start to track, always give your dog as much opportunity as possible to pick up the track's odor right at the start. As previously mentioned, don't kick down the ground surface or shuffle on the track or at the start. Some trainers say that it is necessary to give the start a width of one yard (1 m), but we disagree. If the wind is strong, such a wide start can even be a disadvantage if you want the dog to proceed straight onto the track. Odors move quicker across a large, wide start than they do on a start/track that is three overlapping foot-widths wide. As well, if a wind is buffeting the start and track from one side, a big part of the track's odor will come to rest beside the track, and your dog may start slanting and may miss the track if the start is too wide. The method described above for making a start and track has been proven in practice to work: your dog can easily pick up the odor and move on to work out the track.

To end this chapter, we will discuss the importance of landmarks to laying a straight track and also give you some training tips for tracking.

Landmarks, the Points of Orientation

To develop a straight track, you should, while standing beside the stake, choose a certain point in the far distance and walk toward it.

Make sure you choose a point of orientation that you will be able to identify later, after the track is made. For example, one tree amongst many in a forest will, without doubt, not be recognizable later! Instead, choose a church, a building, a tree standing alone, a fence, or another easily identified point. Note that this orientation point has to be at a distance; it should not occur on the track itself.

When you begin laying a track, start by considering wind direction, terrain, or orders of the judge or your trainer. When you know the direction the track has to be laid, choose the start point. Standing on the starting point beside the stake, choose your point of orientation. As you begin your paces to lay the track, make sure you keep your head up and focus on the chosen point. People who look at the ground as they lay a track will likely change direction and create a track that twists all over the terrain, which makes tracking in a straight line difficult for the dog. As well, if your dog is following a twisty track during a test, the judge may think that he is not secure on the track.

The advantage of a good point of orientation and a straight track, especially as you begin training your dog to track, is that it allows you to determine whether or not your dog is on the right track. Otherwise, it is difficult for you to correctly assess your dog's movements. You have to know exactly where the track is laid, otherwise you might be praising your dog even as he walks away from the track. If a big error in assessment like this occurs more than once, your dog thinks he is doing well when he walks nose to the ground without really tracking. This problem occurs more frequently than you might think. At the same time, you must be very careful not to correct your dog too quickly; he may be on the right track! It is important to have confidence in your dog's nose. We must not think that we, with our poor senses, know better than the dog does.

Training Tips

Most of the mistakes your dog will make as he learns to track are actually reflections of your mistakes. The following training tips should help you avoid common stumbling blocks as you begin to train your dog to track.

First, remember to take your time. You cannot teach your dog to track immediately. Concentrated tracking is a heavy job, and your dog must be up to the challenge, both physically and mentally. Dogs that are too young, too wild, or too slow will need to spend more time on basic exercises, which will give them enough confidence to proceed to the next steps. Trying to teach a difficult, excitable dog to track is hard work that often produces poor results. From the beginning, make sure that retrieving exercises with that old leather glove or other favorite toy are going well and that your dog is enjoying himself. Never force him along by progressing too rapidly.

During training, try to ensure that your voice is always calm and encouraging. Avoid training on days when you are not in a good mood. If you are not feeling positive, your dog will reflect that in his work and track poorly. Leave your dog at home rather than, by responding rashly and unthinkingly, making a mess of your dog's training. The more confidence you have in your dog and the more balance and certainty you show, the better your dog will work out the track. Try to bring out the best in your dog as much as possible, not by punishing him when things go wrong, but instead by anticipating his actions and encouraging him in the right manner with your voice.

Your dog should not have too much food before leaving home for the tracking field. Eating makes people languid, and it does the same for dogs. After eating, blood circulates away from your dog's brain and muzzle toward his stomach and intestines. A feeling of stupor comes over a dog after eating. A just-fed dog just cannot track correctly. Be aware of other physical conditions that might affect your dog's ability to track, things that may not be as obvious as post-meal doldrums. For example, if your dog is in heat, or even a month away from being in heat, she may perform poorly on the track or work out the track with less intensity than usual.

Besides not being full of food, your dog's nose should be in good order before you set out for the tracking field. His nose should be fresh and slightly moist. To ensure a fresh nose on the track, make sure your dog does not wear a flea or tick collar. Flea collars emit a certain odor that could interfere with your dog's ability to smell the track. As well, as you drive with your dog to the tracking field, avoid smoking in the car. Perfume, aftershave, and hairstyling products can also affect your dog's sense of smell. Never transport your dog in the trunk of your car. It is cruel and can lead to your dog inhaling exhaust fumes. The best place for your dog is in the back seat, or in the back of a station wagon or hatchback.

When you arrive at the tracking field, choose a quiet place where your dog's attention will not be easily diverted from the task at hand. Give him some time to get used to the environment and take care of his needs. As you progress through tracking exercises, keep two important things in mind: rest and patience. The tracking field should be peaceful at all times—try to stay away from barking or restless dogs. Allow your dog to explore the area quietly; don't apply any pressure on him to perform. Your dog needs to get used to the tracking field in order to be confident about his actions there. Make sure your dog does not bark at other dogs or people passing by. Talk to your dog in a calm tone and praise him for correct behavior. When you are ready to create the track, turn your tie-out stake into the ground calmly, fasten your dog to the stake without excitement or upset, and leave your dog behind without command. You can practice all of this at home before going out to the field so your dog knows what to expect.

When you set out to make the start of the track, consider adopting the following routine—it works for us! Create a practice of placing your equipment bag—holding your long leash, harness, and stakes—about 11 yards (10 m) from the place where you plan to put the start. Put the bag down and walk the 11 yards straight ahead to the start place; then turn around and walk back to the bag. Remove your start flag or stake and go back to the start area. As you perform this back-and-forth journey, walk normally, using regular paces. Remember never to shuffle or damage the ground. In this manner, before you've even begun laying the track, you've already created a triple track between the bag and the start, leaving your odor behind.

Of course, at the trials, judgment of your dog's ability to track begins at the start, and every mistake you and your dog make will cost you. We often see dogs sniffing intently from the start and following the track to the start's end only to circle back to the beginning of the start. At an exam, the judge will dock points for that kind of behavior. It is okay for your dog to sniff around and double back, but only before it arrives at the start. (It is, of course, best if the dog does not behave this way at all!) When you lay a triple track between your equipment bag and the start, your dog can work out its hesitation without losing points. If you always create this bag–start track during training, your dog will be accustomed to it and it will become part of his routine, too. Making this pre-start area at an exam isn't a problem: you only give the impression that you forgot your flag or stake in your bag. In the end, this little routine reduces your dog's chances of a bad start at a trial because it gives him a head start on sniffing the track's odor.

After you've created the start and laid the track, go back to your dog and praise him for waiting quietly, but don't make him restless by praising too much. If your dog is calm when you return to him, proceed to work out the track directly. If your dog was not lying down quietly when you were laying the track, don't punish him; instead, pet him for a while. (You should be practicing the lying-down exercise somewhere besides the tracking field to get your dog used to staying alone while you create the track.) Try to quiet him by speaking in a calm and friendly way. You may need to spend some quiet time with your dog before you begin investigating the track. By all means, take the time you need to quiet your dog before you begin. As you already know, restless dogs cannot track correctly.

When your dog is ready to track, attach his leash to his collar and take him to the beginning of the track: the equipment bag. As you walk to this point, do not pressure him to follow at heel. When you are near the bag, quietly put the tracking harness on him and then fasten his leash to the harness ring. When you begin training, use a normal leash rather than the long tracking leash.

What comes next is important. As soon as your dog puts his nose to the ground to sniff at the track, praise him: "Good boy!" Praise and rewards for good behavior are of utmost importance for dogs learning to track. If your dog is obstinate, never punish or speak harshly to him, but try to encourage him to do what you ask. There is a difference between "asking" and "commanding." What you "ask" the dog to do is to search, and so you use the word "Search" or "Seek" in a friendly tone, pronounced without any hint of pressure. Draw out the sound of the vowels in the word—"Seeeek"—which demonstrates both a friendly request and a stimulus to search.

2

The Different Parts of Tracking

Preparing for the Test

At an IGP trial, the judge determines the pattern of the track according to the test regulations and considering the layout of the available terrain. Varying patterns can be used for tracks. The judge gives instructions to the tracklayers and observes the laying of the track. The judge may conduct a draw to decide the order in which the participants perform.

The turns and the articles needed for the different tracks may not be situated or laid down at the same places on each track. The start of the track needs to be well marked with a stake, which must be placed in the ground directly to the left of the start. All natural terrain—grass, plowed fields, and forest surfaces—are acceptable for tracking at a trial, but remember to avoid the possibility of your dog tracking with his eyes and not his nose! For all tracking levels, it is possible to adjust the available terrain by change of surface. Bear in mind that while the track is being laid, the dog—and, for IGP 2 and 3, the dog handler—must be out of sight.

The Tracklayer

For the IGP 1 trial, the tracklayer is always you, the handler. For IGP 2 and 3 exams, the tracklayer must be a stranger to the dog,

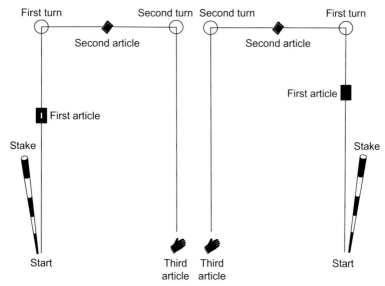

In IGP 1 and 2 exams, the judge often asks you to create a U-form track.

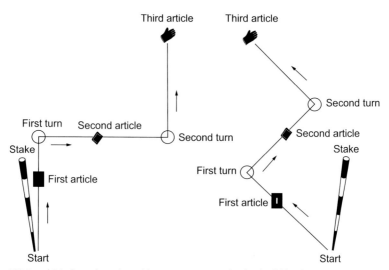

IGP 1 and 2 judges also ask tracklayers to create tracks that look like these.

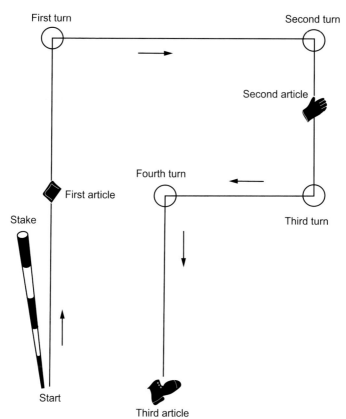

When training for IGP 3 trials, handlers often create the R-form track.

often an experienced tracklayer. It is important for tracklayers to walk at a natural walking pace when setting out tracks. The tracklayer may not provide help to the dog, such as an unnatural walking pace or unauthorized turns or articles. Before walking the track, the tracklayer must show the articles to be situated on the track to either the judge or the track coordinator. Only articles that have been pocketed by the tracklayer (i.e., scented) for at least 30 minutes may be used.

The judge will tell the tracklayer where to lay out the track and how to make the turns. The tracklayer is to remain for a brief time at the start and then proceed at a normal pace in the designated direction. The judge will use a whistle signal to indicate to the tracklayer where he wants articles and turns placed; one whistle blast usually means a turn and two mean setting down an article. The turns (approximately 90° each) should also be walked at a normal pace to ensure a seamless tracking flow that the dog can follow into the next leg of the track. Scuffling or integrating a break in stride is not permitted while conducting turns or laying down the legs of the track. The distance between the individual legs must be a minimum of 30 paces.

Harness and Leash

During the tracking phase of a test, your dog may wear a harness in addition to the chain collar or a Böttger tracking harness. The dog may track free or be attached to a 33-foot (10-m) line. The line may be held over the dog's back, to the side, or between its front and/or back legs. The tracking line may be attached directly to the collar but not to the live ring, or it may be attached to the harness ring (harness or Böttger harness without additional straps). Retractable leashes are not permitted.

Reporting In and Out

The handler prepares the dog for the track by fastening the dog's tracking harness, rolling out the tracking line, and fastening the line to the collar. When called, the handler goes with his dog to basic position and reports in to the judge, telling her whether the dog will pick up or indicate the articles present on the track. Presenting to the judge has to happen in accordance with IGP regulations: "Owner/handler [your name] presents [breed and name of your dog] for IGP 1 [2 or 3], phase A. The dog will indicate/pick up the articles." A good instructor will train you to present so you are ready for it during the examination. After you present, the judge will wish you luck and tell you to begin. It is important that you keep your dog as quiet as possible when you present and during the trial; you should also remain calm. Have confidence in your dog. By the time you come to the trial, he will know what he is doing and will be able to work out the track without fail.

When you are ready to begin, fasten the tracking line onto the tracking harness and start!

After completing the track, the found articles must be presented to the judge. After picking up or indicating the last article, you must report out and receive your points before you play with or feed your dog. Make sure you and your dog assume the basic position (see the obedience section of this book) when reporting out. The report takes place as follows: "Owner/handler [your name] reports out [your dog's name] for IGP 1 [2 or 3], phase A. Three articles located." After you have reported out, take your stake and other equipment away from the tracking field. Be careful that you and your dog don't hinder someone else as you leave the tracking field.

Start

Before you begin, you are permitted to sit your dog briefly, about six feet (2 m) before the start. Then, at the direction of the judge, slowly and calmly take your dog to the start, where he can begin tracking. The dog has to start intensively, calmly and with a deep nose. He must take the scent without any influence from you, except for your brief and normally intoned command to "Track." The start is not under any time constraints; remember that the judge must observe your dog's behavior at the beginning of the first leg and note how intensively he orients himself to taking the scent. Your dog is allowed three attempts at the start to take the scent, after which the track is terminated.

When your dog
starts out on a
track, he should
be calm, intense
in his sniffing, and
use a deep nose.

Tracking

During the trial, the dog has to track with a deep nose, maintain-ing a steady pace. You, the handler, must follow him at a distance of 33 feet (10 m), at the end of the tracking line. If your dog tracks free, maintain a distance of 33 feet as well. There may be some slack in the tracking line, but don't shorten the line and therefore get closer to the dog. It is no fault if the line touches the ground.

The dog must follow the track intensively, with endurance and, when possible, an even speed, depending on the terrain and the degree of difficulty. You are not obliged to follow the course of the track, for instance, at turns. The amount of time your dog takes to finish the track does not affect his rating, as long as the track is consistently and convincingly worked out.

The judge will terminate the tracking if your dog is more than a line length off of the track (over 33 feet [10 m] if he is tracking free of a line). If you stop your dog from leaving the track, you will receive instructions from the judge to follow your dog. You must follow those instructions.

Occasional praising is permitted in IGP 1 trials (the command to "Track" is not considered praise). However, you may only praise your dog when he indicates or picks up the articles. Brief praise may be given either before or after the article is shown to the judge.

Turns

During the test, your dog has to be confident as he works out the turns in the track. He is permitted to check left and/or right beside the track without leaving the track, but circling at the turns is faulty. After executing a turn, your dog has to continue tracking at the same even speed he established before the turn. In the area of the turn, you should maintain the required distance, if possible. Praising is not permitted at the turns.

Articles

As discussed, at a trial, only articles that the tracklayer has carried for a minimum of 30 minutes may be used. Within a given track, articles made of various substances—leather, textiles, wood—may be used. The articles must be approximately 4 inches (10 cm) long, 0.8–1.2 inches (2–3 cm) wide, and 0.2–0.4 inches (0.5–1 cm) thick. The articles must not be significantly different in color from the terrain of the track and must be laid down when the tracklayer is walking the track. After placing the last article, the tracklayer must, according to the IGP guidelines, continue walking several paces, straight forward from the article, before ending the track.

As soon as your dog has found the articles, he has to convinc ingly (and without handler help) either pick up or indicate them.

Remember that your dog is not permitted to play with, move, or pick up the article while he is lying down near it. Such actions are considered faulty at IGP trials.

It is faulty if he picks up and indicates the articles at the same time. If he picks the articles up, your dog may remain standing after doing so, or he may sit or return to you. You must remain standing throughout this part of the process. Your dog may not continue investigating the track with the article in his mouth; it is also faulty if he lies down with the article, or lies down to pick up the article. If your dog begins to return to you after picking the article up, do not move forward to meet him.

If your dog indicates the articles instead of picking them up, he may do this while lying down, sitting, or standing. Alternating between these postures is also permitted. If your dog lies down to indicate the articles, he is allowed to lie in a position that is not completely straight out from the article. However, he may not lie down beside the article or turn around to look at you, the handler. Articles that are indicated with strong handler help are considered to be "overrun." For example, an article would be overrun if your

This handler is raising his arm, article in hand, showing the judge that his dog has found the article.

dog did not indicate the article and you, either by use of the line or through verbal command, hindered your dog from continuing to track. When your dog indicates the article, you must drop the leash and go to him. When you approach your dog, stand next to him before picking up the article. Then, raise your arm with the article in hand, showing that your dog has found the article.

Evaluation

At an IGP tracking trial, the judge expects dogs to demonstrate convincing, intensive, and dedicated nose work, as well as a good training foundation. The judge observes not only the dog and handler but also the tracking area, the weather, possible cross-tracks, and the time it takes for the dog to work out the track. In his evaluation, the judge has to take into consideration all of the following factors:

- Track behavior (the dog's speed on the legs of the track, before and after the turns, and before and after the articles)
- Training status of the dog (i.e., a hectic start, showing pressure, avoidance)
- Handler help
- The dog's ability to work out the track despite:
    - Ground conditions (overgrown areas, sand, change of terrain, fog)

- Wind conditions
- Wild game and game tracks
- Weather (heat, cold, rain, snow)
- Changing weather conditions during tracking

- Dawdling, searching with a high nose, relieving himself, circling at the turns, constant handler encouragement, lacking intensity, boisterous tracking, hunting mice, line or verbal helps within the tracking area or at the articles, and incorrect pick up or indication of the articles, are all faults and evaluated accordingly.

Note that it is not faulty if your dog checks left and/or right beside the track without leaving the track. As well, if your dog follows his hunt drive, you may give the command "Down" to maintain control; track work will continue at the instruction of the judge. If this does not work, the trial is terminated with the evaluation: disqualified due to lack of control.

3

Training with Tracking Equipment

Articles

For IGP 1, 2, and 3, the tracklayer places three articles on the track—not beside it. These articles should belong to the tracklayer (for IGP 1, you, the handler) and can be made of leather, textiles, or wood. The articles should each be about 4 inches (10 cm) long, 0.8–1.2 inches (2–3 cm) wide, and 0.2–0.4 inches (0.5–1 cm) thick. The articles may not stand out in color from the terrain.

When first beginning training, the articles you lay down should always be interesting for your dog, such as items he already commonly retrieves. The dog's search drive will be heightened when he searches for an article that has special meaning. The best articles for tracking are made of leather or wool. However, woolen articles should not be of the brightly colored, thick, sock-ball variety. If articles are visible at the start, dogs will not search for them intensively with their noses. Bear in mind that between leather and woolen articles, leather ones are better because they absorb odors for a longer period, and they are already usually the right colors for tracking—brown or black, similar in color to the tracking field. Old wallets, gloves, or parts of old shoes all work well. If you use such unremarkable articles during training, you are sure to encourage your dog's tracking drive.

Whether used during training or trials, the articles should carry the strong odor of the person who laid the track, hence the importance of putting tracking articles in your pockets before going to the tracking field. Simply put, your dog will not find the articles with his nose unless they are redolent with the tracklayer's odor. You should ensure that the articles are close to you for at least half an hour before laying them on the track, making sure you don't remove them from your pockets until it is time to place them on that track. When they are close to your body, the articles warm up, and that warmth helps them retain your scent. When placing the articles, make sure you do not always lay them in the same order, in the same places on the track, or the same distance from one another. As well, articles should not be placed so close to one another that after finding one article your dog is able to see the next one, prompting it to find articles with his eyes and not with his nose. Especially when you begin training, do not lay the articles too close to a turn, and certainly not right on a turn. If your dog is tracking well, you can change from using familiar articles to unfamiliar ones.

When your dog locates an article, always praise him, "Good boy!" And when he is having trouble locating the articles—or as the trainers say, "has a walk over"—don't be angry. Put the article in your pocket without complaining to your dog. Instead, encourage your dog to continue the search. When the dog has a walk over, don't give up on the training session. Rather, make a short, new track, placing the article he failed to locate at the very end. Start your dog at the beginning of the new track, and a few yards before reaching the article, stand still, give your dog more leash, and wait until he locates the article. Encourage your dog to search and praise him when he searches in the right direction. When he locates the article, it is celebration time for you and your dog: praise him enthusiastically. Never leave the field after a failure; always employ a new, short track so you and your dog can finish on a note of success.

INDICATING OR PICKING UP

When your dog finds the articles on the track, he must make it clear to you that he has located them. There are two accepted ways for your dog to do this: indicating the article by standing, sitting, or lying down in front of it; or picking up the article and giving it to you, the handler. The latter is possibly nicer to see, but it may not be the easiest method to teach. There are many different opinions about the advantages and disadvantages of both methods, but IGP regulations do not distinguish between the methods, so long as the dog points out all the articles in the same way. So, either teach your dog to point out all articles by sitting, lying down, or standing, or by picking them up. Of course, when reporting in at a trial, you must tell the judge how your dog is going to point out the articles.

During tracking training, when you teach your dog to stand—or, more commonly, to lie down—near an article, you may

This Boxer indicates that he has found an article on the track by sitting next to it.

involuntarily put pressure on the dog. You should put no pressure on your dog during tracking. If he is too often commanded "Down" when he finds an article, that command may exert pressure on him. Locating an article is then no longer an enjoyable activity but a punishment. Sometimes, during the first few tracking exercises, dogs freely stand, sit, or lie down at the article, in which case there is no reason to train them to pick the article up. In the end, what is important is that your dog stays at the article and does not walk around it or back to you, because then there is a need for commands and pressure again.

RETRIEVING

We recommend training dogs to pick up articles on the track. When you read the obedience exercises in this book (see Phase B: Obedience) and have trained your dog to retrieve with ease, his ability to track to an article and pick it up will be nascent. If you follow this method, when you begin tracking training, use the same articles you used for retrieving (except for the dumbbell).

Start the first tracking exercises when your dog is already retrieving reasonably well: that is, your dog is flying like an arrow out of a bow to retrieve the article and bringing it back to you with the same enthusiasm. After he is able to find the retrieving article on a track, begin teaching your dog to retrieve other articles that are used in tracking. But for that first foray into tracking, your dog will find it satisfying to locate his familiar retrieving article on the track. The enormous advantage to teaching your dog to locate articles on the track in this way is that he is always directly rewarded when he finds the article he is already crazy about. If you have taught your dog well, he will find it fun to retrieve the article on the track. As a reward for locating the article and retrieving it, throw the article once more for him to fetch. It is incredibly rewarding for you, too, to see how enthusiastic your dog is about finding and then retrieving the article. As your dog goes through more tracking training, only throw the last article your dog finds on the track. When the rascal discovers that only the final article is thrown for retrieval, he will redouble his efforts to locate all the articles on the track quickly and enthusiastically. Most of the time he will discover that the shortest way to an article is by following the right track. You can see that by following this method, you ensure that your dog becomes so focused on the articles that he will do everything it takes to find them. As a result, your dog discovers that his nose is his best friend, and he quickly learns to make that necessary connection between the track and the articles.

At an examination, when your dog has located an article, you may not put it in your pocket. Instead, you must hold the article up high so the judge can see that your dog has found it. During training, however, this part of tracking is done differently.

When you make sniffing sounds with your nose and your dog can hear it, he will react naturally by mimicking you. Try it! When you are training your dog to track, provide encouragement by sniffing along with him as you walk behind him. And sniff when your dog has located an article, too. Sniff clearly, audibly, and in detail at the article and tell your dog what a good boy he is. Then, after you have rewarded your dog, put the article in your pocket and encourage him to move on to the next article. When he has found the last article, let your dog retrieve the article again as a reward. Your dog finds more enjoyment in searching for articles when you are also sniffing for them and at them. He discovers that you, the leader of his pack, are checking his work and are interested in the articles, which in turn stimulates your dog's own interest in tracking. Try this sniffing routine, even if you find it embarrassing. Observe how your dog tries to smell when he hears you sniffing, either visibly moving his nostrils or even clearly and audibly sniffing. We recommend this activity strongly because it provides extra stimulation during tracking training, even if it looks a bit foolish!

Try tracking once this way and you will be amazed at the results. Remember, IGP regulations only allow handlers in IGP 1 trials to briefly praise dogs after showing articles to the judge. However, there are no rules against sniffing! Consider sniffing subtly during an examination.

Tracking Harness and Tracking Leash

From the first time you track with your dog, use a well-fitting tracking harness and a leash. Although IGP regulations allow dogs to track free of harness and line, while teaching your dog to track, it is better to use a correctly fitting tracking harness with a pliable tracking leash. Make a special ritual of putting the harness and leash on before tracking. Your dog will better learn what is expected of him when he trains with a harness. Some trainers still suggest that handlers begin training using a chain collar. However, a chain collar will put undue pressure on your dog: when you jerk at the collar, the dog will think that he is being punished. Tracking harnesses pose no such danger as they are made to cause the least possible hindrance during tracking and yet help handlers keep a line on their dogs. A proper tracking harness is made of good quality leather and has a connection for the line on the dog's back.

There are also tracking harnesses that have rings for the line in front of the chest or the throat. The tracking leash is connected there and then pulled between the dog's front and hind legs, and the handler holds the leash walking behind the dog. As long as you take care not to jerk at the leash, such a harness can be helpful. However, we have seen many handlers who use these harnesses to correct their dogs when they are not tracking properly. They jerk the leash against the dog's stomach and sexual organ, which is cruel. After such treatment, is it any wonder why the dog doesn't learn to track better but instead develops a fear of tracking? Having seen this result too many times, we have come to prefer harnesses whose rings are located on the dog's back.

The tracking harness has to be pliable and should not hinder your dog's movements. Do not tighten it too much; you should be

The tracking harness you use should be pliable and not hinder your dog's ability to track.

able to put your flat hand between your dog's body and his harness. If you have more than one dog, we recommend having separate harnesses for each, adjusted to the right size.

Affix a tracking leash to the back ring of the harness. This leash should be the required length of 33 feet (10 m). Tracking leashes may be nylon, cotton, or leather. Nylon leashes are lightweight, but if your dog suddenly jerks, these lines can easily slip through your fingers and cause injuries. Cotton leashes are much easier to keep in hand, although they are a bit heavier. However, when a cotton leash becomes wet and dirty, it becomes rigid. Tracking leashes made out of thin chromium leather are pretty and pliable. There are also thin, round, leather tracking leashes, which also work very well. Leather tracking leashes are more expensive than their counterparts, but they are pleasant to work with. Regardless of the type you choose, consider wrapping tracking leashes around a small wooden plank so they do not tangle in your equipment bag.

Before you set out, place a knot in your tracking leash at the 10-yard (9-m) mark, or one yard (1 m) before the end of the leash. This way, when your dog walks away from the start and you play the line out through your hands, you'll know that the end of the line is about one yard after the knot.

When choosing a tracking leash, consider the benefits and pitfalls of the different types. Leashes are made of materials such as nylon, cotton, and leather.

Tracking is intense work for your dog, and he should not be hindered by things like a tangled tracking leash or a bad or ill-fitting tracking harness.

Tracking is serious work for your dog, and so he should not be hindered by things like a tangled tracking leash or a bad tracking harness. Roll the leash out before you start so that it cannot become tangled. Keep the leash between you and your dog, always off the ground. If your dog is going to walk around you, drop the leash immediately to avoid becoming tangled in the line.

Other Equipment

Besides articles and a harness and leash, you will need a few other items before you can begin tracking training with your dog, including a bag, a stake to indicate the start, a tie-out stake, and a training log.

You need a bag in which to carry all your equipment. Avoid using plastic bags because on the way to the field a plastic bag can tear or become uncomfortable to carry, and your discomfort with the bag can break your dog's concentration on the task ahead. Instead, consider using a linen bag, a backpack, or a shoulder bag. Backpacks and shoulder bags allow you to walk to the tracking field with free hands.

The start is to be clearly marked with a sign—a colored dowel, a flag, or an iron stick all work well—which must be placed directly in the ground to the left of the start.

A tie-out stake, which looks like a big corkscrew, is a big help when there is no place for you to tie your dog up while you lay the track in the field. The stake has a ring on which you can fasten the dog's line, which allows the dog to turn around without becoming tangled. As you tie your dog up, remember not to pressure him with grim commands; instead, be calm and relaxed. Your dog should sit or stand on the tracking field, demonstrating calm behavior when you walk away to lay the track. (Hint: To protect your equipment bag from the sharp end of a tie-out stake, push a piece of garden hose onto the point.)

Remember to remove your start marker and tie-up stake from the ground when you have finished for the day; farmers can damage their equipment on such stakes, which in turn damages your relationship with farmers. It's important to be respectful of field owners. Remember that handlers need farmers' cooperation to ensure they have tracking fields available for training.

The final piece of equipment you will need before you begin training your dog is a simple notebook in which you can keep track of your progress. In this training log, you should describe all sorts of information:

- weather conditions
- terrain
- wind direction with respect to the track
- length of the track
- amount of time your dog takes to work out the track

- number of articles found and the results of indicating
- the way the dog worked out the track, and so on.

Make notes about everything, and make drawings of the tracks you lay down. When you have a thorough log, you can go back to any of the training sessions and find out how your dog was tracking and what was going wrong or going well. The log will help you and your instructor keep track of your progress and note any weak points that may have to be addressed. Remember to note down information about exercises other than tracking, too. It might seem to be a bit cumbersome, but a log book provides amazing support to your training efforts; if you don't keep track of your activities, after some weeks you will not know what kind of mistakes you made earlier and what the causes were. If you do keep track, you and your instructor can discuss what you have done and find solutions to problems.

4

Tracking with Treats

Your dog's level of motivation and concentration are very important when you are training him to track. So, when you begin teaching a dog about tracking, first ensure that the training environment is quiet, with few distractions. For example, when you first introduce your dog to a track, you don't place a flag, sign, or marker at the start. This would only distract your novice tracker; he would look at it, sniff and touch it, and consequently lose focus on the ground, the track. One way to keep your dog focused on the track from the start is to train him with treats. This method is described here for puppies, but it can also be used if you have an older dog that is just learning how to track.

Training at the Start

The best type of terrain on which to begin tracking training an eight-week-old puppy is arable land. Start your training by making a good track start for your dog. In a 1.5-foot (0.5-m) square, make many little steps with your feet close together. Take your time as you do this to ensure your scent is strong within that square, and finish it off by putting pieces of kibble in your footsteps. While you are laying out this start square, spend most of your time in the center of the square (the area that is four inches (10 cm) away

When you begin training a
puppy, don't worry about
placing a flag, sign, stake,
or other marker at the
start of the track. Such
markers will only distract
your puppy from the work
at hand.

As soon as your dog starts
to sniff in the start square
you've created, command
"Search," saying the word
in a sustained manner:
"Seeaarrchh."

from the edge). This will help your puppy stay within the smell of
the footsteps.

When you have this square laid out and ready, pick up your
puppy, leash him, and go to the prepared area. As soon as the puppy
starts to sniff in the square, give him the command "Search," enun-
ciated in a sustained manner. Make sure he doesn't simply set to
and eat all the kibble right away. As soon as he has found and eaten
about eight to 10 pieces, give a signal—a click of your clicker, for
example—and then, with one or two pieces of the same kibble in
hand, lead the puppy out of the square.

When your puppy leaves the square, he is well aware that there
are some pieces of kibble left behind. Strike while the iron is hot,

and set to work making another start square in the same manner described above, and repeat the procedure with your puppy. In this new square, the puppy will enthusiastically search out the pieces of kibble. Repeat the square routine three or four times during your training session, each time removing the puppy before he has eaten everything with a clear command, such as "Ready? Good boy," "Finish," or "Free."

The kibble-strewn square exercise should be repeated between 20 and 30 times over your next few training sessions before you and your puppy can advance to the next step in training, which involves the same basic method, but with a smaller square and a different kind of treat. (Remember: the treat you lay on the ground should always be the same as that which you carry in your hand at the end of the exercise.) You can also work on other soil surfaces, such as a meadow with short grass. Don't consider advancing, though, until your puppy obviously understands the process and likes searching around in the start square. The next step should also be practiced 20 to 30 times over the course of a few training sessions.

Training with the Treat Ball

When you are not training your puppy in the start square, spend some time at home showing him how to play with a little ball that releases treats when it rolls slowly. Your young dog will not only be delighted with the rewards that fall out of the ball, but he will also learn to move the ball very slowly, because the treats only come out when the ball is rolling slowly. Every time you work with this ball, change the type of food or treats you use. As soon as your puppy understands how the treat ball works, you can use it when training in the square.

Begin by burying the treat ball in the start square, but first make sure your puppy isn't watching you! Because the puppy has already learned that the ball must roll very slowly before treats will come out, it will also dig that ball out very slowly. This activity makes for a slow but intensive and concentrated dog working out the start square. After the puppy has dug up the treat ball 20 to 30 times, slowly and with concentration, you can begin encouraging it to work out other shapes on the soil. Instead of a 1.5-foot (0.5-m) square, for example, walk out a 1.5-foot- (0.5-m-) diameter circle. Incorporate the buried treat ball straight away. As you progress with the new start shape, reduce the diameter, just as you reduced the size of the 1.5-foot treat-strewn square. After employing a circle, create a triangle, then a pentagon or an oval; experiment with different shapes on different types of terrain.

Concentration on Footsteps Is the Key

When you begin training a puppy to track with the above exercises, it is important that he learns to concentrate at the start. When a dog is able to concentrate on taking in the odors of the footsteps at the start, he is more likely to continue along the track, employing the same level of concentration from start to finish.

The main principle to follow as you train your puppy is that concentration on footstep odor is the key to good tracking. The puppy should not learn to track the food you lay down. Yes, he finds food in the human footsteps, but the footsteps should be the focus. For this reason, it is crucial that you use several types of kibble or food when practicing the above exercises. This way, your puppy will not focus on the treats but on the footsteps, which are leading him to the food.

Remember not to use a play ball or toy when tracking training with a puppy; ball play will cause your puppy to slip into a high drive, which will hinder his learning. When tracking, the puppy should instead learn to be highly motivated but in a low drive, employing a high level of concentration. This can be accomplished by asking your puppy to search at the start for the buried treat ball described above, to then dig it out and as a reward eat the treats that come out when the ball is slowly rolled around.

Training with Articles

At first, the articles you will later place on the track for your dog to find must be introduced to your puppy somewhere besides the track. The first order of business with the articles is to teach your dog to lie down with them upon finding them. As mentioned previously, tracking articles must be approximately 4 inches (10 cm) long, 0.8–1.2 inches (2–3 cm) wide, and 0.2–0.4 inches (0.5–1 cm) thick. They are usually made out of leather, wood, or a kind of textile—they are never balls or toys. Remember, too, that the articles' color must blend in with the colors of a tracking field.

After pocketing an article for at least 30 minutes, remove it and hold it briefly in front of your dog's nose. Then, push the article between his forelegs. Your dog will lie down because he wants to sniff at the article, and he will concentrate on the article because it smells interesting. As soon as your dog is lying down, immediately reward him with food. Repeat this exercise many times so he understands that when you give him an article, he must then lie down with it correctly placed between his forelegs.

When you are training your dog to lie down in front of the article on the track, push the article between his forelegs. Because he wants to smell the article, his nose will follow it and he will lie down. As soon as he is lying down, reward him with food.

When your dog understands this oft-repeated procedure, change the exercise up a bit by throwing the article on the ground instead of placing it between his forelegs. He should lie down right away. If the article is not in between his forelegs, help him to lie down correctly, but do not give him a reward. Only offer a reward when your dog lies down correctly all by himself, with the article in the right position. Bear in mind that if your dog consistently needs help positioning the article, you may have progressed to this step too quickly. If this is the case, go back to the previous exercise and repeat it a few more times before attempting to throw the article again.

Training to Track

The preliminary exercises described above can be performed with your puppy until he is between five and six months of age. At this point, it is time to start tracking! Ensure you have all the equipment you need to begin, and always work with your dog in a harness and on a leash. Begin by laying a track that is only a few paces long, extending it outward every time. As you begin this next step in training, consider the following suggestions.

Try to avoid laying monotonous, straight tracks. Instead, create tracks that bow in different directions. On a straight track that has rewards at its end, your dog will inevitably track too quickly and not remember to concentrate. On a bowed track, your dog has to pay attention. As well, varied tracks keep the exercises interesting for dogs. So, to ensure that your dog is highly motivated to track, keep your training consistent and your tracks various.

When laying out your many and various tracks, don't put kibble or food on the surface of the ground in the footsteps. Instead, place the treats in a hole made in the tip of the footstep, or press the treats into the soil with your shoe. This way, your dog has to use his nose to sniff around in the footsteps to find the treats.

Begin training your dog to track turns by first laying a straight, 6.5-foot (2-m) track that ends with a small curve. Create this curve

If you are using treats to train your dog to track, place them in little holes at the tips of your footsteps when you are laying the track, or press them into the soil using your shoe.

Variety in training leads to a highly motivated dog on the track. Switch up the surfaces you train on, too, from meadows to tilled fields.

by taking small steps. When your dog is successful in investigating this track, create a similar one, but make the curve sharper. Repeat, making the turn sharper still. As you and your dog progress, consider introducing him to an older track, or a longer track, or a track with more or fewer articles and turns. When your dog reaches the end of the track after finding the last article, always take his leash off and give him a food reward.

5

Tracking with Toys

The First Short Track

When training with toys, the first training track we lay for a dog is a straight one, about 50 paces long, in a dewy (morning), short-grass meadow. You will have placed the tracking article in your pocket at least a half hour before laying the track, so it should be covered in your odor. Keep the article in your pocket while you tie your dog to the tie-out stake, and then pick up your equipment bag and walk over to where you will lay the track. Your dog is allowed to see what you are doing from a distance, but he has to be quiet. While laying the track, don't react to your dog and don't give commands. Pay close attention to the condition of the terrain, and choose where you want to lay the track, making sure that the wind will be at your back.

After you've walked out the bag to start track we described in the first chapter under Training Tips, create the start by placing the stake into the ground at your left side, choosing a point of orientation, and then walking straight ahead with small, overlapping steps about 13 feet (4 m) straight ahead. At that point, take one step to the side and walk back to the stake in the same way. Upon reaching the stake, turn and walk straight back toward your point of orientation. Begin by using short steps, and then lengthen the distance between them after the first 13 feet, slowly progressing to larger paces that are about the same length as your normal stride. Do not walk quickly at the beginning, but as you begin to take larger steps, increase your speed to a normal walking pace. Take care that in the beginning you are laying a track replete with odor. While walking on the track, keep your head up and look toward your point of orientation so you don't deviate from your projected track. Walk between 40 and 50 paces straight ahead in this manner, and then remove the article from your pocket and lay it down on the track (don't throw it down beside the track). After you lay down the article, stand still for a moment to leave a bit more odor on that spot. (Later, you can lay the article down normally on the track as you walk.) Then, walk some paces forward at the same tempo, and then turn and walk a very wide circle back to your dog. If there are other tracks on the field, instead of circling back, walk to the end of the field and return to your dog along the field's outskirts, thereby avoiding walking diagonally through other tracks.

Once you have collected your dog, walk with him over to the equipment bag and put on his tracking harness and the normal leash. Then stand beside your dog, place your hand a short distance before his eyes, and indicate toward the ground, holding your hand still for a moment above the track. At the same time, say, "Seeeek," and encourage him to follow your hand with his eyes. Do this a number of times as you step forward alongside your dog, the leash slack. If your dog brings his nose to the ground, praise him: "Good boy!" If he doesn't do that, encourage him once again with a friendly "Seeeek." This is the way you walk forward, bending over beside your dog, encouraging him to use his nose. Remember not to touch your dog or the track with your hands, but walk quietly and encourage him: "Seeeek, good boy." Using a calm voice, keep your dog close to you, but don't pull on the leash. And don't apply pressure if your dog does not want to put his nose to the ground, but keep trying to get him to follow your hand movements with his nose, and stimulate his sniffing instinct by doing some sniffing yourself. In this manner, follow your "bag to

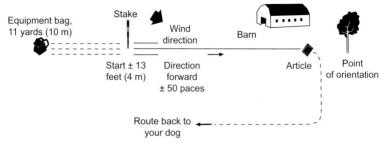

Equipment bag, 11 yards (10 m) | Stake | Wind direction | Barn | | Point of orientation
Start ± 13 feet (4 m) | Direction forward ± 50 paces | | Article |

Route back to your dog

The first track you create could look something like this. Put your equipment bag down about 11 yards (10 m) from where you make the start. Before laying the track, make sure you have a distinct point of orientation, in this case, the solitary tree. You will also want to mark where you place the article on the track—here, the back of the barn indicates where the tracklayer has placed the article. After placing the article, walk in a wide arc back to where your dog is quietly waiting for you.

One way to train your dog to use his nose on the track is to first stand beside him and then place your hand a short distance before his eyes. Move your hand toward the ground, holding it still for a moment above the track. Your dog's nose will follow your hand.

start" track and make your way slowly to the start, where you have ensured there is a lot of odor.

By the time your dog reaches the start, he has possibly already put his nose to the ground a few times, after which you will have praised him: "Good boy." At the start, walk on very quietly, taking small steps. If your dog puts his nose to the ground a little bit, encourage him and see if he continues to use his nose without the extra stimulation of the movement of your hand. If your dog is still not using his nose, calmly proceed, slightly bent forward beside him. Avoid the impulse to become frustrated or impatient if your dog is not reacting, and do not pull on his leash. If he wants to bring his nose up, use your hand to quietly indicate the track, repeating the movements and the encouragement "Seeeek."

Be patient.

As you approach the article, become quieter still, and do not put pressure on your dog. If he clearly smells or sees the article, let him move along quickly, and follow at a faster pace, leash in hand. If your dog locates the article, it is celebration time for both of you! Praise your dog exuberantly for locating the article, which he will bring to you in his mouth. Sniff clearly and audibly at the article yourself when you take it from your dog. As a reward, throw the article and let him retrieve it. After that, put the article in your pocket.

If your dog is having trouble finding the article, stay in its vicinity, make sniffing sounds, and ask your dog to search. Say, "Good boy" if he puts his nose to the ground and tries to smell. Sniff along with your dog until he has found the article. Do not pick up the article. Instead, encourage your dog to pick it up. Never kick articles around on the track or move them in any other way after they have been laid down. Always let your dog search and use his nose to find articles, even if it takes some time. As well, make sure you always celebrate when your dog finds an article. After you have exaggeratedly sniffed at the article, let your dog retrieve it, and then, with a lot of praise for your dog, put it away.

At this point in the training session, release your dog's leash from the tracking harness and fasten it to the collar chain again. Your dog will come to realize that this action indicates the end of tracking. He will learn that he must find the article before tracking ends. As well, he will learn that upon finding the article he will receive a reward (retrieving the article). Rest assured that after the first few successful attempts, your dog will learn what is expected. It is very important that these first tries are enjoyable for your dog, so really try to make the context as ideal as possible. After the first successful attempt, do not immediately lay more tracks, but go off the tracking field to take care of your dog: let him have a drink, relieve himself, and play for a while.

Before you leave the field, do not forget to remove your start stake and tie-out stake.

In the beginning, practice tracking once every two days with your dog, working only on a straight track unless your dog is running too quickly over a straight track, in which case you should lay bowed tracks. Always make it interesting for your dog, and motivate him to use his nose by praising him and sniffing along with him.

Your Dog Is Tracking!

When your dog is using his nose more readily, it is not necessary to continue to move your hand before his eyes to help him pick up the scent of the track. At this point, it is important to ask your dog to work—"Seeeek. Good boy."—and encourage him to use a deep nose to follow the track and locate the article.

When your dog is readily using his nose to track, you do not have to continue making motions with your hand above the track.

The word "Seeeek" encourages your dog to track, and "Good boy" offers praise when he is using his nose. If your dog is tracking well, say nothing more than those two phrases so that he can concentrate on the task at hand. You may also wish to say "Good boy" once while your dog is locating the article. Otherwise, your dog has to learn to track with concentration, and you should not divert him.

As you train, walk behind your dog over the track you laid. When your dog is succeeding consistently, you can exchange the short leash for a 33-foot (10-m) tracking leash. First use only 10 feet (3 m) of it and follow your dog quietly at that distance. If he is staying correctly on the track, you can slowly let the leash slip to 33 feet. A 10-foot leash helps you prevent your dog from straying too far from the track; a 33-foot leash does not give you this option. If your dog wanders too far away from the track, you can correct him with a calm "No" followed by "Seeeek." If he returns to the right track, praise him with "Good boy."

Never jerk the leash to keep your dog on the track. Your dog has to learn to track of his own volition, not in response to jerking and pulling on his leash. Your role is to guide your dog after having laid a solid foundation for tracking. Once on the track, your dog has to work on his own without influence from you, the handler. Remember that a slack leash can be a hindrance, too. Don't let the leash behind the dog drag over the ground during tracking. The part behind you may drag over the ground, of course, but not the part between you and your dog.

We cannot stress enough that training your dog to work out a track involves slow buildup. It may help you to remind yourself frequently about your two-part goal: 1. Your dog learns to use his nose and locate articles; and 2. Your dog learns how to soundly work out the track.

If tracking is going well, you can change up the exercises to increase your dog's skills. For example, raise the time limit of the track slowly from five to 20 minutes or longer. Also consider lengthening the track. From a 55-yard (50-m) track, progress slowly to a 164–219-yard (150–200-m) straight track. While you are at it, augment the tracking exercises by adding a second article—one at half way and one at the end of the track.

Another way you can challenge and sharpen your dog's tracking ability is to lay out a track that is buffeted by the wind on one side; but only do this when you have consistently observed your dog tracking correctly and with a deep nose. Before laying down such a track, pay close attention to your dog and try to get him to the point where he keeps to the right track, thereby easily locating the articles. After that, tracking against the wind will not be a problem, but don't start introducing your dog to such tracks too early. There is a danger that your dog will too easily find the odor of the track in the air and will then track with a high nose. Then, your dog could start tracking with a high nose regardless of the wind conditions, which will cause problems in the future when he has to make turns.

Indicating

If your dog stays at the article the first few times he finds it— standing, sitting, or lying down—don't pressure him to retrieve. Drop the line, go to him, and praise him enthusiastically. Don't forget to sniff at the article for a moment. Never use pressure to make your dog lie down if he is standing at the article. His behavior can be corrected later, when he is tracking well.

Pay attention to your dog's tail while he is tracking. The tail can tell you a lot about the dog's mental status. With his tail a dog can tell you if he is happy or afraid, uncertain or resolute. A tracking dog's tail can also tell you if he is aware of an article nearby. The dog's tail will change position from stiff hanging during tracking to wagging after smelling the article, or the other way around.

Turns

After working out a straight track correctly, without deviating from it, your dog is usually ready to investigate a track with a turn. Make the start as you've already done, first ensuring that the wind is affecting the side of the track, and lay out the first leg (at least 55 yards [50 m]). Don't lay an article on this first leg of the track.

At the spot where you want the track to turn, stand still for a moment and then make a 90° turn to the left or to the right (into the wind) and then walk along to create the second leg. When you are between 30 and 40 paces from the turn, lay the article down.

After laying this track, collect your dog, fit him with his harness and long leash, and begin, walking quietly behind him. As your dog walks over the turn, he will lose the smell of the track. As soon as you know this has happened, stand very still and remain quiet. Let your dog work it out on his own. Eventually, give him a bit more line, but don't push the line to send him in a certain direction. Stand still and wait. Let him search quietly for the track. If your dog puts his nose in the air, encourage him: "Seeeek." Your dog might then circle as he searches for the odor of the track. In such instances, never call your dog back to you or work in with the leash, but let him search carefully. Eventually encourage your dog with "Good boy." It may take a while, but he will find the turn and the second leg of the track, and you will be rewarded for your patience. When your dog has found the second leg, praise him in a quiet tone and then let him continue searching for the article. The wind—for you have laid the second leg so that after the turn your dog is working against the wind—often helps your dog to quickly find the second leg. If he hesitates on the turn, he will easily catch the odor of the sideways track. At the turn, walk as quickly as possible behind your dog and cut the bend. After that, walk behind him on the track.

Another way you can introduce turns to the track is to make a curve or bend, then narrow that curve over time until it becomes a straight turn. The problem with this method is that a bend can divert your dog because he has to cope with a series of small shifts in wind direction instead of a single, abrupt change. Dogs that consistently investigate tracks with intensity will not have a problem with a turn. They already know how to use their nose and will thus simply search busily around the turn for the second leg.

The dog's nose truly
is a wonder!

Be patient as your dog works out the turn; refrain from using the tracking leash to draw him around the corner. Rest assured that once your dog works out one turn very well, more than one turn on the track will not be a problem. First, however, practice on a track with one turn a few times. Every time you make this track, place the turn at a different distance from the start. The first time, place the turn at 11 yards (10 m), and then make a turn after 55 or 109 yards (50 or 100 m). You can also vary wind direction, the number of articles on the track, turns to the left and to the right, and so on. Variety is the key to preventing your dog from becoming used to a pattern. If possible, try to get your dog used to tracks laid under fences, through different types of terrain, and near buildings to provide even more variety. Another way to change things up is to lay a track that begins on one type of terrain (perhaps a meadow) and ends on another (for example, a ploughed field).

If at any time your dog is having a hard time working out a complicated track, make a straight track in ideal conditions and let him investigate that. It is okay to take a step back in training now and then. Your support and a solid training foundation and buildup to new and different tracks are the keys to your dog's success and enjoyment. Your patience is also essential.

When a one-turn track is a piece of cake for your dog, lay down more turns and add variety. Always note your experiences in your training log, and check that you are not making the same mistake over and over again. As well, remember that dogs often become bored or frustrated with tracking because their handlers or trainers are overtraining them. Watch your dog for signs of frustration and adjust your training schedule as needed.

Excitable Dogs

If your dog is prone to running the track, you can slow him down by speaking to him calmly. Avoid drawing in the leash. It is important for dogs to learn to track slowly and quietly so they are able to find articles and negotiate turns. When you speak quietly to slow your dog down, he may lift his head. Follow up with a quiet "Seeeek" and "Slow," and then let him continue along. Never put too much pressure on excitable dogs that are just learning to track. Later, your dog's drive to run will decrease when he has to work out difficult tracks that have more turns, more articles, are buffeted by wind, and are older and so not as easy to sniff out. Of course, you can also make bowed tracks, which also help keep excitable dogs from running the track.

Slow Dogs

If your dog is working slowly and a bit unwillingly, you should first find out if your dog is physically unwell. If your dog's health is not the cause, you may be applying too much negative pressure on him. For example, perhaps you are trying to teach your dog to heel and sit correctly in anticipation of when the instructor or judge asks you to present for tracking. In doing so, you may be applying too much negative stress on your dog. Let up. Instead, try to stimulate your slow dog with an encouraging voice, and try to make him more attracted to the article by, for instance, retrieving fun at home. Dogs with low interest in tracking are rare. Again, the cause is usually too much pressure from the handler and poor handler-dog relations. If you are having trouble, try to stimulate your dog with praise and improve your relationship with him by spending a lot of time with him. If this is not successful, a track of treats, as described in the former chapter, can be helpful.

Training for IGP 2

If the points you earn during the IGP 1 examination are not particularly high and you gained your diploma by the skin of your teeth, we advise you to do that trial again to get a bit more experience. You can repeat a trial as many times as you want, and it's worth it to have a good foundation before moving on to IGP 2. Tracking in the IGP 2 exam is more than just a follow-up to IGP 1. In IGP 2 examinations, your dog must work out a longer, older track that is laid out by a stranger. The stranger laying the track is the biggest change for the dog; the rest of the tracking conditions follow from the IGP 1 trial. If your dog has had some difficulty with a track laid out by you, replete with your odor, again, consider redoing the IGP 1 exam and boosting your points before you move on. To prepare for IGP 2, you must first get your dog used to tracking a stranger's scent. Begin this process by asking someone your dog knows and loves to lay the track, and then work up to having a stranger lay it for you.

The "strange" tracklayer begins by laying a track using the same methods you used when training for IGP 1: she will choose a point

During the IGP 2 tracking trials, your dog must work out an older, longer track that was created by a stranger.

of orientation and then lay a straight track. The tracklayer has to clearly remember where she has laid the track so she can escort you during the exercises. She has to be able to ascertain whether or not your dog is still on the track and give you information about the track's development. Begin exercises with a track of about 55 yards (50 m), without turns but with an article belonging to the tracklayer placed at the end. The tracklayer should also lay out a good start where your dog can pick up enough scent to begin tracking.

Work out the track as you have always done in the past. Collect your dog quietly, fasten his tracking harness and leash, and go together to the start. Make sure you haven't been on the tracking field before you take your dog there, otherwise you may confuse your dog with your scent. At the start, give your dog time to pick up the scent. Stimulate him to follow the strange odor with a gentle "Seeeek." Your dog should understand what this means by now, and he will use his nose to follow the track. Praise your dog softly, "Good boy," for his correct insight. If your dog does not understand what to do, go back to how you began working out an IGP 1 track. Walk beside your dog with your hand in front of his eyes, making movements with your hand toward the track and saying the same, soft-spoken "Seeeek." Continue this way until he understands what to do. If, however, your dog knows what is expected of him and is tracking with his nose firmly on the ground, walk a short distance behind him. When he locates an article, celebrate!

Keep training on a straight track until your dog is clearly, sometimes audibly, sniffing deeply and tracking intensively. When your dog is ready for a challenge, add more articles belonging to the tracklayer, then some turns. Let the turns vary as much as possible with the wind direction so that your dog can work out the track correctly under all conditions. Remember to regularly change your tracklayer, thus ensuring that your dog is working with many different tracklayer smells.

When your dog finds the article, reward him by throwing the article for him to retrieve.

Training for IGP 3

In the IGP 3 exam, the track is longer than it was in IGP 1 and 2; as well, the track is left to age for a longer period before the dog is allowed to investigate it. If you did well in your IGP 2 exam, you should be able to train for IGP 3 without a problem. Again, as you train, regularly change your tracklayer and the type of ground on which you are tracking. Don't make your tracks in the same pattern every time. The R form, for example, is very popular with a lot of trainers, who often train it without making changes, which is a big mistake. As you head into IGP 3 exams, make your training tracks as difficult as possible, but raise the degree of difficulty slowly. Take care to study the IGP testing regulations so you know exactly what is required at the exam.

As always, there is no shame in taking a step back in training when your dog is having trouble. Backsliding happens, but how far it goes depends on your reaction to your dog. Your dog should genuinely enjoy his work, and if he sometimes does not work as well as he could, refrain from reacting negatively. Always reward your dog when he works for you. Even during bad times, your dog still has to hear that you are pleased he is tracking. Don't make the mistake of thinking you are above making mistakes, even if you have more experience than the handlers around you. Instead, set an example of how a good handler-dog team behaves. The handler should always be satisfied with the dog, even when the results are poor. Show your satisfaction even as you investigate what might be going wrong. Remember that your dog's work on the track may be going sideways because you are overtraining and not providing enough variety on the track. Also remember that IGP 3 dogs need to be played with, too! Engaging in normal, fun, pressure-free contact with your dog will keep him happy and also happy to work with you on the track.

Phase B

Obedience

6

Obedience Basics

Before we talk about the obedience exercises in the IGP program, we want to talk a bit about dog training methods in general. First of all, compulsion training is not necessary. We now have modern techniques that help us teach dogs the IGP exercises and allow them to learn. Learning manifests in an organism as a permanent change in behavior that is a result of that organism's interactions with the environment. In the case of dog training, there are three important types of learning that we will discuss here: classical (Pavlovian) conditioning, operant conditioning, and habituation.

Today, most dog trainers employ classical—also called Pavlovian—and operant conditioning. Dogs perform well when they are trained using these methods, and they learn very quickly which behaviors bring them rewards and pleasure. The third type of learning is called habituation, and dogs begin habituating themselves to their environments from the moment they are born. Through habituation, dogs learn what to pay attention to and what to ignore. (You can read more about the modern methods of dog training in Resi Gerritsen, Ruud Haak, and Simon Prins's *K9 Behavior Basics: A Manual for Proven Success in Operational Service Dog Training*.)

The foundation for success in the IGP program is a strong working relationship with your dog that is based on respect and communication.

Classical and Operant Conditioning

To be a successful dog handler in the IGP program, you not only have to develop a good relationship with your dog, but you must also understand how dogs learn. For example, your dog needs immediate feedback about her actions in order for her to understand what she has done well (or not well). A dog that has demolished the seats of the car while her owner has popped into the grocery store, then falls asleep while waiting, will not understand what her owner is yelling and shouting about when the owner returns to the car. Immediate feedback is crucial to a dog's understanding of her actions, and it is at the base of the following types of conditioning.

CLASSICAL OR PAVLOVIAN CONDITIONING

When you employ classical conditioning, your dog learns that there is a relationship between two stimuli. One of the stimuli is called "neutral" or "conditioned" and is usually represented by the sound of a clicker or a bell. Normally a dog does not pay attention to the noise emitted by the conditioned stimulus, so called because only as a result of conditioning will this stimulus generate a behavior. The other stimulus, "unconditioned," is biologically important to a dog and is usually represented by food. Dogs will pay attention to food without being taught to do so.

Russian physiologist Ivan Pavlov discovered the power of conditioned and unconditioned stimuli accidentally during a study with a dog. He placed a dog on a table, and then he rang a bell, after which he immediately gave the dog food. After repeating this exercise a few times, Pavlov discovered that ringing the bell made the dog salivate: in the dog's mind, the ringing bell predicted food. Today, you use a clicker (rather than Pavlov's bell) and food or another reward, such as a ball, when you wish to employ classical conditioning when training your dog. Dogs trained in this method quickly learn that a click sound ushers in a reward of some kind.

Modern positive reinforcement training has replaced Pavlov's bell with the sound of the clicker coupled with a food or toy reward.

OPERANT CONDITIONING

When employing operant conditioning to train your dog, you use four methods to influence your dog's behavior: positive reinforcement, negative reinforcement, positive punishment, and negative punishment.

If we want a dog to behave a certain way more often, we use positive reinforcement by giving the dog something it likes, thereby increasing the likelihood that the dog will behave that way again. For instance, if you want your dog to sit, you give her a treat as soon as she sits. She will sit more often because she likes receiving a treat.

Negative reinforcement can also be used to increase the likelihood that a behavior will occur again. Instead of adding something positive to the dog's environment (the treat, in the example above),

If you want to encourage certain behaviors in your dog, use positive reinforcement techniques. If you want your dog to sit, give her a biscuit as soon as she sits.

you introduce something the dog perceives as negative. For example, if you want to stop your dog's incessant barking, you could make a terrible noise as soon as barking commences and only stop when the barking stops. Negative reinforcement is the principle behind stop-barking collars: when she barks, a dog wearing such a collar is either subjected to an unpleasant smell or shocked by an electrical impulse. The moment the dog stops barking, the unpleasant smell or shock stops. Bear in mind that certain deployment of negative reinforcement is not clear enough for the dog to learn what the desired behavior is. For example, trainers and handlers used to jerk on choke-chains to teach dogs to stop pulling on their leashes and to heel in the correct position (shoulder in line with handler's leg). However, many handlers did not jerk the leash in the "right way," so the dog continued to pull and heel incorrectly. In such cases, the dogs did not understand the negative reinforcement. Today, trainers and handlers teach dogs how to heel using a different method, as is discussed in the next chapter. So, we will not talk about what would be the "right way" of jerking a leash because nowadays it is not the right way to train a dog.

Operant conditioning also includes two types of punishment, positive and negative, which we use when we want to discourage certain behaviors.

With positive punishment, you add something aversive to your dog's environment to discourage a behavior: an unexpected, unpleasant noise when the dog barks, for example. Because it surprises and annoys the dog, the noise will cause the dog to stop barking. As she learns that the noise starts up every time she barks, your dog will bark less to avoid hearing the noise. As well, a handler might discourage a dog from chasing other dogs (or rabbits or other animals) by throwing a chain on the dog's back as soon as she starts to chase. In similar circumstances, some handlers put an e-collar around the dog's neck and shock the dog as soon as it starts up a chase. This type of punishment was often used in earlier days of dog training, and sadly some trainers and handlers continue to employ such methods. Happily, some countries now forbid the use of prong or pinch collars and e-collars.

The last method used in operant conditioning to decrease the frequency of certain behaviors is negative punishment: removing something the dog experiences as pleasurable. For example, if you do not want your dog to jump up on you, don't pay attention to her when she jumps. If she tries to get your attention in a way you do not like, ignore her until she behaves in a way that you like. Then, take notice of your dog to reinforce the good behavior!

Habituation

From the moment your dog was born, she has been surrounded by stimuli that she must get used to and learn from. She soon learns to distinguish between the sounds, smells, sights, and tactile stimuli that she should attend to, and those that are not important. After all, any organism's nervous system would be overloaded if it reacted to all environmental stimuli. For example, in a certain neighborhood, every morning at 7:00 a.m., a newspaper is delivered by a boy who rings his bicycle bell after throwing the paper. A dog living in that neighborhood hears that bell every morning, but no one in her house receives the newspaper. When the dog first heard the bell, she barked, but after a while she noticed that nobody in the house reacted to the bell, so she dismissed the bell as unimportant. For that dog, the bell caused neither an aversive nor a pleasurable response; she just became used to it.

You can make use of habituation in two ways when you are teaching your dog, by either flooding or desensitizing your dog.

When flooding, you present a stimulus full force with no corresponding response from you until your dog stops reacting to it. In this way, she learns to ignore the stimulus because the stimulus has no consequences.

When desensitizing, you first present the stimulus quietly, at a low level, and gradually heighten the experience of the stimulus. When your dog is habituated to this stimulus, she will be desensitized: all experiences of the stimulus (from low to high) will not provoke a response. For example, some dogs are trained to ignore the sound of a shotgun by using desensitization. You begin by exposing your dog to the sound of a shot fired far away, perhaps when you are playing with your dog. Then, you gradually decrease the distance from which the shot is fired until someone can shoot a gun 65 feet (20 m) from your dog and not provoke a response in her.

We use habituation when training dogs for obedience in the IGP program. For example, when teaching your dog to sit, you begin by choosing a training space that lacks distractions: a room in your house or in your garden. When your dog has practiced the exercise a few times, you can move the "classroom" to a place where there are more distractions, such as a dog-training center at a time when dogs are absent. Remember that the smell of other dogs is already a distraction! If your dog is able to perform the exercise correctly every time when the training center is quiet, you try taking her there to train when other dogs are present.

Clear Signals in Training

We have learned that dogs learn skills best when they are offered rewards like treats, a game of ball or tug, or even permission to repeat a behavior or trick that the dog likes to perform. In addition to giving rewards, you should use cue words to communicate clearly with your learning dog. The cue word could be "Yes" or "Free," or you may instead use a clicker to indicate to the dog that she has done well, but can stop now. In the beginning, rewards should immediately follow appropriate behavior. The combination of clear and consistently used cue words and rewards help dogs to learn when they are doing the right things. Communicating clear signals during training is incredibly important.

Remember that before your dog understands the cue word, you must teach it to her by uttering the word in combination with a reward, much like Pavlov's bell-food experiment. Your dog thus learns that the cue word means "Okay, stop, and food." The

Handlers and trainers use cue words to give dogs direct feedback: "You are doing the right thing!"

moment she hears the cue word, she knows she will get a reward. In the beginning the reward should be food; later, you can reward your dog with a game of ball or tug.

The combination of cue word and reward is a positive one for dogs and worth employing as you take your dog through the IGP obedience exercises. Your dog will want to practice the exercises again and again because of the rewards. For you, the handler, this method is also satisfying because you know you have established a clear channel of communication.

As in tracking training, it is also important in obedience training that you do not follow a set pattern, day in and day out. Change up the timing of rewards—for example, if you have been working on the Down Under Distraction exercise, change the amount of lying-down time, first 10 minutes, then three, then 15. Variety is your dog's friend in all training exercises, and so it is also a boon for you because your dog will be enjoying herself.

Punishment

Sometimes your dog will not do what you want, and so you must correct her. First, ask yourself, "Did I teach my dog this behavior? Is this a behavior that needs to be corrected?" If the answer is yes, you can choose between three methods of "punishment": positive punishment, negative punishment, or time out.

To be effective, positive punishment must be immediate and strong enough to suppress the unwanted behavior. Also, the punishment must be deployed in a way that ensures your dog associates it only with the unwanted behavior. The punishment must elicit a response every time for it to work; that is, your dog must respond to the punishment by stopping the inappropriate behavior. For instance, perhaps your young dog likes playing with other dogs and during training the Heeling exercise she runs to another dog to play. You could at this point grab her by the neck and shake her a bit, and say a very powerful "No."

Negative punishment gives your dog the opportunity to self-correct. Note that dogs will do whatever they can to be rewarded. If you notice that your dog is not performing an exercise correctly, such as sitting, you can apply negative punishment by withholding a reward and saying "No." After saying "No," say, "Sit" again, and if your dog responds correctly, give her the cue word and reward. Your dog has already learned that following the cue words is a reward. If one of her actions does not lead to the cue word and reward, she will try to figure out what she has to do to get the reward again.

Finally, you can also use a time out to correct your dog's unwanted behavior. This is a good option if your dog is over stimulated or distracted and is not able to concentrate on the work. However, bear in mind that time outs only work when your dog wants to train.

Correcting dogs by using pinch collars and electronic collars is old fashioned and not recommended in IGP training. Some trainers and handlers still use these tools, even if they are forbidden by law. However, if a dog handler uses a pinch collar or electronic collar on a dog before, during, or after an IGP trial, that handler will be disqualified.

7

Obedience Exercises

The obedience exercises are divided into nine parts at IGP level 2 and 3 trials. At IGP 1 trials, there are eight obedience parts because participants do not have to present the Stand exercises. The total number of points you can earn during an obedience exam is one hundred.

When you are at the obedience phase trials, judges are particularly attuned to the relationship between the dog and her handler. The handler should not pressure the dog, and the dog should demonstrate a fine level of self-confidence, which in turn shows that the dog is no mere piece of "sporting equipment." During all exercises your dog should display a happy work ethic and the concentration required to successfully complete her tasks. Following are the nine exercises required of your dog during the obedience exams.

Exercise 1: Off-leash Heeling

Exercise 2: Sit in Motion

Exercise 3: Down with Recall

Exercise 4: Stand while Walking (IGP 2) or Stand while
Running (IGP 3)

Exercise 5: Retrieve On the Flat

Exercise 6: Retrieve Over a Hurdle

Exercise 7: Retrieve Over the Scaling Wall
Exercise 8: Send Out with Down
Exercise 9: Down Under Distraction

Basic Position

Before teaching your dog any of the above exercises, teach her the basic position because every exercise starts and ends with it. In the basic position, the dog sits straight up on your left side in a calm and attentive manner with her right shoulder blade level with your knee (or hip if the dog is large, ankle if the dog is small). During the trials, you are only allowed to give a single command to your dog to assume the basic position. While the dog takes the basic position, you, the handler, must stand straight with straight legs held together, arms down at your sides. A splayed stance is not permitted for any exercise.

At the start of IGP trials, you and your dog should assume the basic position as another handler in the arena takes up his position with his dog at the Down Under Distraction exercise area. When both teams are in position, evaluation happens simultaneously. Brief praise is permitted at the end of each completed exercise, which in turn is followed by assumption of another basic position. Only three seconds is allowed to elapse between giving praise and starting the next exercise.

Exercise 1: Off-leash Heeling

In Off-leash Heeling, only one verbal command—"Heel"—is permitted. You may give this command at the start of heeling and when changing pace. At the start of the IGP 1 trial, approach the judge with your dog on leash (for IGP levels 2 and 3, approach with the dog off leash). Ensure your dog sits as you report in. When the judge dispatches you, proceed with your dog at heel to the start position. When the judge gives further instructions, you may begin the exercise.

For this exercise, from a correct basic position, your dog has to follow you on your left side at the "Heel" command in an attentive, happy, and straight manner, with her shoulder blade in line with your knee, and she must sit straight, independently, and quickly when you stop walking. At the beginning of the exercise, you and your dog advance 50 paces without stopping. During this first leg, two shots (6-mm caliber) are fired within a time-frame of five seconds and at a minimum distance of 15 paces. Your dog must show impartiality to the gun shots. If she shows gun shyness, she will be disqualified and all awarded points will not be recognized.

After an about turn and an additional 10 to 15 paces, you must begin to run then slow up, 10 to 15 paces of each, using the "Heel" command at each transition between running, slowing up, and walking. Execute the transition from the running pace to the slow pace without intermittent steps. After this leg of alternating speeds, walk on at a normal pace and demonstrate at least two right turns, a left turn, and an about turn, as well as a stop after the about turn. Throughout the exercise, your dog must keep her shoulder blade aligned with your knee and stay on your left side; she may not forge ahead, lag behind, or heel wide.

You and your dog must demonstrate the about turn (a 180° turn in place) in one of two possible manners. You can either turn in place with your dog turning behind you to the right, or, you can both make a left about turn by turning 180° in place. At a trial, only one of these is permitted.

At the end of the exercise, you and your dog must walk into a group of at least four moving people. You have to maneuver left around someone, right around another, and then stop once in the middle of the group. The judge may request a repeat if he thinks the dog has a weakness in her temperament. At the instruction of the judge, you and your dog leave the group and assume the basic position. This basic position marks the beginning of the next exercise.

When heeling, your dog must start in a correct basic position and then follow you, her handler, at the "Heel" command in an attentive, happy, and direct manner. While heeling, her shoulder blade should be aligned with your knee.

Development Phase

All of the IGP obedience exercises flow out from the basic position. After the basic position there is a development phase, in which you and your dog take at least 10 paces (15 maximum) together before you give the command to execute an exercise. As well, between all fronts and finishes—and when you return to your sitting, standing, or lying dog—a distinct pause of three seconds is required. When you need to return to your dog, you may approach her from the front or go behind her. Mistakes made in assuming the basic position and the development phase are evaluated accordingly.

Exercise 2: Sit in Motion

For this exercise, you are allowed to give your dog one verbal command each to "Heel" and to "Sit." Begin in basic position with your dog off leash, looking straight forward. In the development phase of this exercise, which happens during the first 10 to 15 paces, your dog has to heel in a straight position at your knee in an attentive, happy, quick, and concentrated manner. After the 10 to 15 paces, your dog is to immediately respond to your "Sit"command facing the direction you have both been facing, without you having to break stride, change pace, or look back. After you have advanced 15 paces from that command, stand still and then turn to face your calm and attentively sitting dog. At the instruction of the judge, return to your dog and stand on her right side. Remember, you can approach your dog either from the front or by going around behind her.

Exercise 3: Down with Recall

When performing Down with Recall, you are allowed to give one verbal command each to "Heel," "Down," "Here," and "Finish." You begin this exercise in straight basic position with your dog off leash, looking straight forward. In the development phase, again the first 10 to 15 paces, your dog has to heel in a straight position at your knee in an attentive, happy, quick, and concentrated manner. After the development phase, your dog has to respond to "Down" immediately and facing the direction in which she was moving with you, without you having to break stride, change pace, or look back. After advancing 30 paces from the command, stand still and turn toward your calm and attentive, lying dog. At the instruction of the judge, recall your dog either with "Here" or by speaking her name. Your dog must then come to you happily, quickly, and directly, and then sit close in front of you, looking right at you. Finally, you may give the command to "Finish," at which your dog has to quickly move into the basic position, either by walking behind you and to your left, or from the front.

If your dog has learned how to lie down properly, she will have the foundation she needs for the exercises Down with Recall and Down Under Distraction.

Exercise 4: Stand while Walking (IGP 2)

During this exercise, you are allowed to give one verbal command each to "Heel," "Stand," and "Sit." In Stand while Walking, you move from a straight basic position with your dog off leash, straight on. After 10 to 15 paces, your dog is to immediately respond to the "Stand" command. You must advance 15 paces, then stop and turn around to face your quiet and attentive, standing dog. At the direction of the judge, return to your dog and take up position on her right side. After approximately three seconds, at the instruction of the judge, your dog is to sit quickly and straight at the "Sit" command.

Exercise 4: Stand while Running (IGP 3)

For Stand while Running, you are allowed to give one verbal command each to "Heel," "Stand," "Here," and "Finish." In this exercise, you and your off-leash dog must begin with a straight basic position and then set straight out at a running pace. After 10 to 15 running paces, your dog must respond immediately to "Stand" without you having to break stride, change pace, or turn around. After you advance 30 paces from your dog, stop and turn around to face your quiet and attentive, standing dog. At the direction of the judge, recall your dog either by the command "Here" or by speaking her name. She must come to you happily, quickly, and directly, and sit close and straight in front of you. At the "Finish" command, your dog should take up the basic position again.

Exercise 5: Retrieve On the Flat

Weight of Dumbbells Used in IGP Trials

Exercise	IGP 1	IGP 2	IGP 3
On the Flat	650 grams	1,000 grams	2,000 grams
Over a Hurdle	650 grams	650 grams	650 grams
Over a Scaling Wall	no dumbbell*	650 grams	650 grams

*Note: In IGP 1, the dog only climbs over the scaling wall; no retrieving is required.

For this exercise, in IGP 1 exams, your dog must retrieve a 1.4-pound (650-g) wooden dumbbell, in IGP 2, a 2.2-pound (1,000-g) wooden dumbbell, and IGP 3 a 4.4-pound (2,000-g) wooden dumbbell. You throw the dumbbell approximately 33 feet (10 m) out from where you and your off-leash dog are in basic position. When the dumbbell comes to a stop, you may issue the command "Bring." You may not move from your position. Your dog should respond to "Bring" by going out to the dumbbell quickly and directly, picking the dumbbell up and bringing it back to you, quickly and directly. She then has to sit close and straight in front of you and must hold the dumbbell calmly in her mouth until you, after waiting about three seconds, command, "Out." You then take the dumbbell from your dog with both hands. Hold the dumbbell calmly in your right hand with your right arm along the right side of your body. Finally, on your verbal command to "Heel," your dog must quickly assume the basic position. Throughout this exercise, you are not permitted to move from your standing position.

Exercise 6: Retrieve Over a Hurdle

In this exercise you begin by assuming the basic position a minimum of 13.1 feet (4 m) in front of a 3.3-foot (1-m) hurdle. From the straight basic position, throw the 1.4-pound (650-g) dumbbell over the hurdle. Your calm and off-leash dog should be sitting next to you. When the dumbbell comes to a complete stop, give her the command "Jump," at which point she should advance to the hurdle and jump it. While your dog is jumping over the hurdle, give the command "Bring." She must jump over the hurdle quickly and run directly to the dumbbell, pick it up immediately, turn back, and then jump back over the hurdle and bring the dumbbell directly and quickly to you.

The dog must sit close in front of you and hold the dumbbell calmly in her mouth, ready for your command, "Out," spoken about three seconds after she has sat down. Take the dumbbell with both hands, then hold it in your right hand with your arm hanging down along the side of your body. Finally, ask your dog to "Heel," and she should quickly assume the basic position. As in the previous exercise, you may not change positions during the course of this exercise.

Note that if you throw the dumbbell too far to one side of the hurdle or if it lands in such a way that it is difficult for your dog to see it, you may ask the judge for a re-throw, or the judge may ask that you throw the dumbbell again.

When jumping the hurdle, your dog must move quickly and not touch the hurdle.

Exercise 7: Retrieve Over a Scaling Wall (IGP 2 and 3)

For this exercise, assume the basic position with your off-leash dog at least 13.1 feet (4 m) in front of the 70.9-inch (180-cm) scaling wall. From this position, throw the 1.4-pound (650-g) dumbbell over the wall. Your dog should remain calm, sitting next to you until you give the command "Jump," after which she should advance directly to the wall and scale it. When she is scaling the wall, command, "Bring." After scaling the wall, your dog must run quickly and directly to the dumbbell, pick it up, and return, climbing back over the wall to bring the object to you. When she returns, your dog must sit close in front of you and hold the dumbbell calmly in her mouth, ready to present it to you when you give the command "Out" three seconds after she has sat down. Hold the dumbbell calmly in your right hand with your right arm hanging at the side of your body. Finally, ask your dog to "Heel," and she should quickly assume the basic position. Again, you cannot change positions during the entire exercise.

Note that if you throw the dumbbell too far to one side of the wall or if it lands in such a way that it is difficult for your dog to see it, you may ask the judge for a re-throw, or the judge may ask you to throw it again. If a re-throw is performed, your dog must remain in the basic position until commands are given.

In the retrieve exercises that employ the hurdle and the scaling wall, your dog must find and retrieve a dumbbell weighing 1.4 pounds (650 g).

In IGP 1, the dog only climbs over the scaling wall; no retrieving is required.

Exercise 8: Send Out with Down

When performing this exercise, start in the basic position and then walk with your off-leash dog straight out in the designated direction. After 10 to 15 paces, give the "Go out" command while simultaneously raising your arm and standing still. Your dog must go out in a goal-oriented way: in a straight line and at a quick pace, advancing a minimum of 30 paces in the designated direction. At the judge's instructions, give the command "Down," and your dog must immediately lie down. Keep your arm raised until your dog is lying down. At the direction of the judge, go out to your dog and

During Send Out with Down, walk forward 10 to 15 paces before standing still, raising your arm, and asking your dog to "Go out." You must remain in that position while your dog goes out quickly, as directed, a minimum of 30 paces in a straight line. Then, she must lie down promptly when you command "Down."

position yourself on her right side. After approximately three seconds, and at the instruction of the judge, give your dog the command to "Sit," and she should quickly assume the basic position.

Exercise 9: Down Under Distraction

At the trial, before the beginning of another dog's obedience exercises, you and your off-leash dog proceed to a place assigned by the judge. This place is usually on the side of the training field, and the host organization will have marked male and female places where you give your dog the command "Down." She should go down and stay without you having to leave a leash or another article with her. As soon as your dog lies down, you must leave her without looking back and advance about 30 paces away from her within the trial area. In IGP 1 and 2 trials, you should always be visible to your dog, but with your back to her. In the IGP 3 trial, you advance about 30 paces out of your dog's line of sight. In all the trials, your dog has to remain calmly lying down without any encouragement from you. At the same time, the dog and handler that are beginning their exercises will perform exercises 1 through 8 nearby. At the instruction of the judge, you may return to your dog and stand on her right side. After further instruction from the judge, and after a three-second pause, ask your dog to "Sit" and thus assume the basic position.

In the next chapters we describe the methods and tools used for teaching dogs the exercises described in this chapter. We are confident that the methods we describe allow dogs to learn how to present the exercises happily and with concentration during the IGP trials.

8

Basic Position and Off-leash Heeling

The Basic Position

Every new exercise starts and ends with the basic position: your dog should sit straight and close to you, on your left side, in a calm and attentive manner. Her shoulder should be aligned with your knee. It is worth it to train your dog to assume the position correctly because during an IGP trial, every time she assumes a correct basic position, she earns points!

There are several methods you can use to teach your dog the correct basic position. Handlers used to teach this position by putting the dog on a leash and then pulling up the leash in front and pushing the dog down in the back. This method forces the dog into the position, and as a result the dog tries to avoid assuming the basic position because she does not like the pulling and pushing. Today, we use other methods when training a dog to take this position; the one you use depends on whether you are training a puppy or an older dog.

TRAINING PUPPIES

Start teaching your puppy the basic position by first putting her on leash and then palming a piece of food in your left hand. Step forward with your puppy on your left side, ensuring the puppy is close to your left leg. Stop and place your treat-laden left hand over her head, which will cause her to bend back to look at your hand, which in turn will make her sit down. As soon as she sits, say your cue word—"Yes" or "Good" or "Ready"—and give your puppy the piece of food. Repeat this several times. However, do not give the food to your puppy if she is sitting crookedly or somehow askew, otherwise you are rewarding the wrong position. If you only reward her for taking up the right position, your puppy will make a habit of sitting properly.

Another way to teach a puppy to assume basic position is with the incentive of a piece of cheese held in your left hand. Position yourself so your puppy is standing in front of you and is able to smell the cheese. Let her nibble on the cheese that extends between your thumb and forefinger. Then, use your left hand to trace a half-circle on your left side, from your front to behind you, with the puppy following your hand. Then turn your hand quickly around and let the puppy nibble again, but this time on the other end of the cheese. Next, place your left hand on your left leg at the spot where the puppy's shoulder should be in basic position. The puppy will move into correct basic position. Repeat this training tactic several times before you add a command. (You can also use this training technique to teach older dogs the correct basic position.)

For both of the above methods, when your puppy knows how to assume the basic position, and is happy doing so, you can slowly stop giving her treats. Ask her to stay in the position longer and longer before saying the cue word and giving the reward. As well, for both methods, once your puppy understands how to take up the position properly, you can speak the command "Heel."

At the IGP exams, when dogs assume basic position, they need to concentrate and look at their handlers, even as they sit close to them. It is very important that the dog feels positive about taking this important position, and so the training must

Employ a treat like cheese to train your dog to take up the basic sitting position. First, hold the cheese in your left hand, and then turn that hand in a circle on your left side, from in front of you to behind you.

After you've turned your hand, enticing your dog and also lining her up, place that hand alongside your leg in such a position that your dog must sit in order to eat the cheese.

be positive, too. Only reward the perfect position. If you do not have a helper to tell you how your dog looks as she takes the position, train in front of a big mirror, either inside or outside. As well, try to avoid getting in the habit of giving body-language hints or other aids—you will not be able to provide hints at a trial.

TRAINING OLDER DOGS

Teach your older dog to assume the basic position before you feed her. Take her bowl of food and stand in front of a mirror or a window so you can see your reflection. Put the bowl on a table next to you, first taking some kibble in your hand. Bring your dog into the correct basic position by taking a bit of food in your left hand and moving the dog into the position. When she sits, give the command "Heel." If she is doing well, say the cue word and give her the kibble. Then, say, "Free," and after a few seconds repeat the exercise: say, "Heel," and wait to see if your dog will assume the correct position. If she does not know what is expected, use the kibble as an incentive. After a few seconds, say, "Free," and after another short break repeat the exercise. When your dog takes up the correct position all by herself, give the cue word, lift up her food bowl, and give her some kibble, then put the bowl back. Again, repeat the exercise, if necessary several times, until your dog truly understands what is expected. If you are consistent, she will learn quickly. Remember: never reward a crooked position and always give the same cue word before the reward. Repeat this exercise every time you feed your dog. You can even portion out her usual amount of food over the course of the day and thereby practice the exercise several times a day.

When you use this training technique, your dog has to work for her food, which has a pleasant spinoff effect. She will start to show a will to please you and cooperate better. As you train this exercise, you and your dog begin to build a solid foundation of teamwork, which is paramount to obedience.

When your dog knows how to assume the correct basic position, begin to teach off-leash heeling. Take a piece of cheese in your left hand and step forward half a pace. Your dog will follow closely because she wants to take the basic position again in order to receive her reward.

Off-leash Heeling

After you and your dog have perfected the basic position, you can progress to heeling. Off-leash Heeling is the most important exercise in the IGP program: all of the obedience and defense-work exercises require dogs to show correct heeling, and even between the exercises, dogs must heel correctly.

When performing the Off-leash Heeling exercise, you and your dog have to demonstrate that she can heel in a variety of circumstances: straight; at slow and fast speeds; during left, right, and about turns; and when walking in a group of people. In principle,

At a trial, even when you and your dog are between exercises,
your dog must demonstrate the correct heeling position.

your dog only has to know that she must maintain the heeling
position in all these situations, but this is not always easy!

BEGINNING TO LEARN CORRECT HEELING

Before your dog can learn to heel, she must first know how to
assume the basic position, which is the position she needs to
take when she heels. Take some food in your left hand and take
some steps forward. Your dog will follow and try to assume the
basic position so she can have her reward. If the position she
takes is correct, speak the cue word and reward your dog. When
she is able to get it right every time, try taking one step to the
side and asking her to assume the basic position. If that goes
smoothly, you can then make a 90° turn and your dog should
follow you to maintain the basic position. As always, repeat this
turn many times so your dog knows what is expected. Vary your
movements during training sessions to keep the training fresh
for your dog, always ensuring that she consistently assumes the
position correctly.

When you are able to take one step forward and your dog heels, try moving forward two steps, then three and four. However, after you've practiced with three steps, go back to two steps before trying four. Progress slowly and in front of a mirror so that you can check your dog's position each time. As well, in the beginning stages, remember to always train your dog to heel in a low drive and with food, so she is not hyper and therefore unable to learn the exercises. Usually food does not make dogs hyper; it helps you bring your dog to attention and into the desired position.

HEELING REWARDS
Once your dog is heeling correctly over the course of 10 to 15 steps, consider switching the dog's reward from food to a ball or another toy. Dogs with low or middle drives may become more focused when heeling with the possibility of retrieving a toy in sight. As well, switching the reward is one way of ensuring that the training does not slip into a routine that becomes boring for your dog. The rewards should always be interesting and offered at a variety of moments during training: sometimes when your dog is heeling and sometimes when she takes the basic position. If you reward your dog when she is heeling, make sure you offer the reward at different times, not always on the eighth step, for example.

There are so many reward possibilities: balls on ropes; magnetic balls, which you can put on your training vest; soft balls; tugs; and so on. If you want to vary the rewards, which we recommend, choose a few toys to use. Remember: the reward should always be something she likes. Before introducing a toy in training sessions, play with your dog and the toy, moving it very fast and throwing it. It will not take long before your dog loves the new toy and you can incorporate it into the training process.

Begin by putting the ball or toy in your armpit. Ask your dog to take the basic position and then slowly move your right hand toward where the ball is. Your dog will catch sight of the ball, and the first few times you do this, she will focus on the ball. To reward this focus, speak the cue word and then let the ball fall down for her to retrieve. After repeating this exercise several times and your dog remains focused, try taking one step and then drop the ball, but only if your dog is in the correct heeling position. Do the same with other toys that your dog likes to play with.

Magnetic balls can be helpful rewards if you've inadvertently made a habit of using body language with your dog to get her to take the basic and heeling positions. You can put these balls on your training jacket in several positions, perhaps on your back, high or low. These balls help dogs "unlearn" your body-language cues because they can pick their reward off your jacket themselves, and you can make a point of standing very still.

Another way to reward with a toy is to hold the toy in your right hand. When you ask your dog to "Heel" and she correctly takes the basic position, speak the cue word and then throw the ball to your left and behind your dog. This manner of reward can help dogs that don't focus well on the basic position or sit too far forward; you will find that the backward fetch will encourage your dog to sit and heel farther back.

HEELING AT TURNS

At IGP trials, your dog can demonstrate the about turn (180°) in two different ways, but you must choose just one of those ways to employ throughout the exam. While you execute the 180° turn in place, your dog must either walk behind you with a right turn, or turn left in place 180°.

If you choose the first possibility, you are at a slight disadvantage in that you will not be able to see your dog while she is turning right behind you. As well, it is difficult to teach a dog to walk closely around you; often she will not walk close enough. If you instead ask your dog to turn left in place alongside you, you will have the advantage in that you will be able to see your dog all the time and ensure she is in the correct position. However, the problem with this choice is that your dog must be able to turn the back of her body and keep the front part of her body in place.

When you begin teaching your dog to turn, start by assuming the basic position and then turning 90° before asking your dog to "Heel." If she follows you correctly, speak the cue word and offer the reward. Repeat, repeat, repeat, varying left and right turns. Your dog will learn to stay close during the turn, whether you are moving right or left. When she can execute the turn perfectly, try moving forward a few steps and then making the 90° turn. You may wish to give your dog a signal that you are about to turn. Of course, such a signal is not allowed during a trial, but you can remove this cue from training once your dog has perfected turns.

To train for the left about turn—in some countries called the FCI or IGP turn—position your dog so that her front paws are on a low, small table. Stand beside your dog and make a step to the right as you say, "Heel." Your dog will follow; ensure that her front paws remain on the table (i.e., she should only move her hindquarters). A piece of food in your left hand, offered at the end of a successful attempt, can be your dog's incentive to do what is expected. By training for an about turn this way, the dog learns to move her hind legs without moving her front legs. Note that some dogs do not need to practice turns with the table to be able to execute a proper 180° turn, but if you find your dog is having some difficulty with the in-place turn, consider incorporating the table exercise before attempting to teach her to turn while heeling.

If your dog does not have trouble turning 90°, you may start turning 180° after a few paces of heeling. Keep some food in your left hand, and use that hand to guide your dog to turn in place by placing your hand in front of your dog. If your dog is heeling correctly and is inclined to remain that way, she will turn her hindquarters and execute the 180° turn. Make sure you offer a reward as soon as your dog completes the turn successfully.

HEELING THROUGH A GROUP

The Heeling exercise requires you and your dog to move through a group of people. You must move to the right around a person, to the left around another person, and then stop once amidst the group of people. To be prepared for the first two actions within the group of people, make sure you train your dog to heel while going in circles, both to the right and to the left. When circling right, watch that your dog does not fall behind you. When you practice circling, you will figure out what speed you need to walk to ensure your dog stays at heel. You will probably discover that your speed is especially important as you circle right because of the dog's tendency to fall behind when heeling in this direction. However, when you circle left, you must ensure you are not moving too slowly.

As you train your dog to heel while circling, put cones or other obstacles on the training field. Later, as your dog gains confidence with the exercise, ask a group of people to be the "obstacles." At first, ask these people to stand still; then, as you and your dog become successful, ask the people to move on the spot. While heeling in the group of people, your dog needs to be focused, concentrating on you at all times.

Markus Mohr and his Malinois Blade von gelben Jewel demonstrate how dogs must focus and concentrate on their handlers the entire time they are heeling within the group of people.

CHANGES IN TEMPO WHILE HEELING

During Heeling exercises, you need to show the IGP judge that you can change your tempo, or speed, without a problem. Start by walking at a normal pace, but after the turn and 10 paces on the way back, increase your tempo. You are allowed to give one command at this point; your dog's position at heel should not change, but she needs to pick up the pace to keep up with you. After 10 to 15 paces, give another command to slow down, and again your dog has to remain at heel as the tempo changes. After yet another 10 to 15 paces, give the command for normal-paced heeling, and again your dog should adjust her pace to match yours (i.e., back to a normal walking speed). This should not be a difficult series of movements, as long as you taught your dog how to do this after she was already a solid heeler at a normal pace.

To teach your dog to heel through tempo changes, first say, "Heel," and then set out normally for a few steps before slowing down. This should be no problem for the dog. Speed up a bit if you find she is executing every step in the basic position. Also, ask someone to observe you and your dog and provide feedback. It will not take long for your dog to understand that she must heel correctly, regardless of your speed. When you feel she is ready, you can add the command "Heel," pronounced slowly when you are moving slowly, normally when you are moving at a normal speed, and quickly if you are moving quickly.

Train your dog to heel at a fast pace in the same way you trained her to heel at a slow pace. Begin with a normal speed, then up the tempo and ensure she maintains the correct position. As you begin to train your dog to heel at different tempos, do not advance too quickly because—especially when training your dog to heel at a fast tempo—your dog may become overly excited. At the risk of repeating ourselves: always teach your dog new exercises in a low drive. So, only advance two or three steps when changing to a quick tempo, rewarding your dog immediately for success-fully maintaining the proper heeling position. If your dog becomes

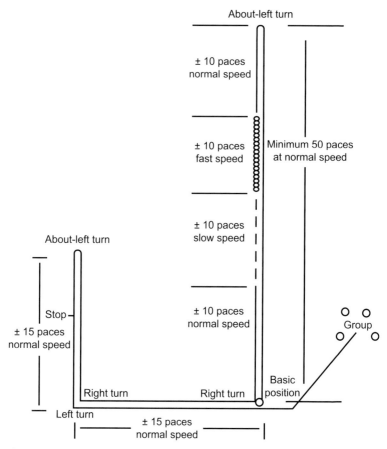

This is the heeling pattern for IGP levels 1, 2, and 3, as is outlined in the *International Utility Dogs Regulations*. The starting basic position also marks where your dog must take up the basic position at the end of the exercise. When you come to the group of people, you and your dog must move around one person from the left side and one person from the right side, and you must halt once near a person of the group.

excited even when you limit the number of steps you take, consider working with food in your left hand so you can keep your dog in position by gesturing with that hand.

Getting Used to Shooting

During training you will notice if your dog minds the sound of a gun firing. You will know right away if your dog is gun-aggressive (displays aggressive conduct in response to the sound of gunshot).

Aggressive conduct in response to gunshot will be evaluated during IGP trials when the judge assesses your dog's temperament. On the other end of the spectrum, if your dog is gun-shy, she will immediately be disqualified with no points awarded. Now before we proceed with ideas on how to train your dog to get used to shooting, what does "gun-shy" mean? If gun-shy, your dog might display one, some, or all of the following behaviors in response to a gunshot:

- She gets up, shows fear, and runs away.
- She runs to you, her handler.
- She shows panic and fear, and tries to leave or leaves the area.
- She shows panic and fear, and runs wildly around.

In the IGP exams, dogs must demonstrate that they are not bothered by the sound of gunfire. If your dog displays any of the above indicators of gun-shyness during an evaluation, the judge will try to determine if the behavior is the result of training errors or a simple coincidence that has occurred during the trial, the result, for example, of the handler accidentally stepping on his dog's toes at the same time the gun is fired. Sometimes the judge will ask the handler to hold his dog on a loose leash and request that additional shots be fired from a distance of 15 paces. If the dog does not react during this second round of firing, the judge will determine that the dog is not gun-shy. In this case, the dog will lose points in the Down Under Distraction exercise, but she will not be disqualified. If, however, the dog still shows gun-shyness during the second round of shots, she will not receive any points and will be removed from the trial. Gun-aggressive behavior, on the other hand, will result in lost points in the Heeling or Down Under Distraction exercises, but a gun-aggressive dog is not disqualified unless she attacks someone or another dog in the field.

Start considering the shooting portion of IGP training and trials from the moment you choose your puppy out of her litter. First, make sure you are buying a puppy that comes from working lines—find out who the parents are and how they have done in IGP trials or in other working disciplines. If you choose to start training an older dog for IGP trials, test her response to gunshots straight away.

To test your dog, take her to a familiar place and play with her for a while so that she is comfortable. Ask two helpers to accompany you to this place: the first person should stand with a 6-mm alarm gun at least 55 yards (50 m) away from where you are playing with the dog; the second person should be observing the dog. The second helper should give the first a signal, upon which that helper will shoot the gun once and then again after five seconds. If your dog does not react, proceed with IGP training. If she reacts by looking up but then resumes play, you know you will have to train her for the shooting portion of the exercises. However, if your dog stops playing and expresses fear, you know she has a problem with shooting and should not be trained for IGP trials. Although there are sometimes ways to work out such a dog's fear of shooting, remember that her disposition is likely dictating her response, and training her not to react to gunshots will be difficult.

For our purposes, let's say you have a dog or puppy with a neutral response to the sound of gunshots. Begin training this dog by habituation to the sound. During training, ensure there is some controlled shooting going on in the background. In the beginning, have someone fire shots as you play with your dog until she ignores the sound. Later, when your dog knows how to heel, have a helper fire two shots while you are practicing heeling. Start with the gun firing about 44 yards (40 m) away, and then reduce the distance to 16 yards (15 m).

Throughout this habituation training, make sure that your dog connects the sound of gunshots to the training field. The dog's perspective should be thus: while she is at the training ground, she is practicing exercises she enjoys with you and her ball or tug toy; other dogs are training, too, and strange people are milling around, and there is shooting. With habituation, she will get used to the

To get your dog used to the sound of gunfire, ensure there is controlled shooting taking place while you train your dog. Here, Lydia Mohr and her Doberman Katie show it is possible to remain focused on training even when a gun is firing in the distance.

complicated context of the training field, and therefore the sound of shooting should not present a problem. Later, when you are at a trial, your dog will not react to the shooting when she is performing the Down Under Distraction because gunfire is part of the training context she knows so well.

9

Sit, Down, and Stand Exercises

Today, handlers use several different methods to teach dogs to perform the Sit, Down, and Stand exercises. Your may start your puppy out in a pleasant and relaxed way, perhaps using a table to teach all three of these exercises. The advantage of working on a table is that your dog learns not to move forward when she is assuming a position. As well, the table must be small enough that your dog will not be able to walk around on it. She shouldn't be able to crawl forward when in the Down position, either, and she should not start performing the Down position from the Sit position. The dog should lie down in one fluid movement from a standing position. As you will see, working on a small tabletop will help your dog learn how to assume the positions without making any unnecessary steps or movements.

Working on a Table

Put your puppy or young dog on top of a small table. Make sure she likes the table and feels comfortable up there. The table's surface should not be wet or slippery. While doing table work, you may wish to employ a clicker; clicks come to indicate desired behavior and are easier to execute than cue words. (Later, when you are training the positions separately, you can exchange clicks

Use a table and a clicker to train your dog to sit, stand, and lie down.

for cue words.) When you are working with your dog on the table-top, you will also want to have some food—perhaps a long strip of cheese—in your left hand.

Once your dog is comfortable on the table, hold your closed left hand up above her head. Your thumb and forefinger should be up. Your dog should follow the movement of your hand and sit down, much as she will do when you train her to assume the basic position (see the previous chapter). If necessary, move your hand back over your dog's head a bit until she sits. As soon as she sits down, click the clicker and give your dog some of the food in your hand, but do not yet link a command to the action.

After your dog has sat down properly and received the reward, turn your left hand around in front of your dog's head, then open up your hand a bit. Your dog will stand up, because she wants to eat the rest of the treat out of your hand. As soon as she stands up, click and let your dog eat.

Now, from the standing position, bring your dog into the down position. Again, palm some food in your left hand, turn your palm down and open it a bit so that your dog could reach the food if she puts her nose down under your hand. Now, put your hand on the tabletop and move it between your dog's forelegs. She will lie down, following the food in your hand, and as soon as she does so, click and give her the reward, opening your fingers one by one.

When teaching your dog to sit on the table, take a treat in your hand and then hold it as shown above your dog's head. The moment she sits, click and give her the reward. Do not add a command to this training exercise until she understands what is expected of her.

Now, to encourage your dog to return to standing, take another treat in hand, then turn that hand in front of your dog's head and open your hand up a bit. Your dog will stand because she wants to eat the treat out of your hand. As soon as she stands up, click, and reward her with the treat.

To teach your dog to lie down from a standing position, palm a treat and then partially close your hand around it. Turn your hand so the back is up (palm down) and open your hand so your dog can reach the treat from underneath. Place your hand down on the table and slide it between your dog's forelegs. She will lie down to get the treat; click and reward her.

Repeat these exercises on the table over and over again, but change the sequence of the positions. Try to avoid training too often from the Sit position into the Down position because you do not want your dog to associate Sit with Down and sitting before lying down: Down is its own, distinct movement.

Combining the Command with the Position

When you are sure your dog can assume all the positions quickly and with confidence, start speaking the command for the position as soon as she takes the position. The sequence of training events should be the following: hand movement, command, click, reward. The next step is to train your dog to maintain the position a bit longer before receiving the food reward. When she can stay in position for a bit before being rewarded, take a few steps back— half a yard or so—from the table while training. Progress by gradually removing your hand signals from your training sequence: from giving the hand signal every time before giving the command, try first giving the command followed by the hand signal, if necessary. At first, your dog may need the hand signal, but it won't be long before the command is enough instruction, which is good, because at IGP trials, hand signals and body language are prohibited.

As always, progress slowly. Remember that puppies and young dogs may need to repeat every training exercise at least 20 times before they are ready for the next step. And those 20 repeats should not be completed in one training session! Each training session should consist of no more than three repeats, and always stop training for the day on a successful note.

When your dog requires only your command to take up a position, try to change your position relative to her during training. First, work in front of your dog, and then stand at the side of the table with your dog on your left. As well, try to give the commands without looking at your dog. Even though your dog is used to you facing her, she must become accustomed to having you at her side. At IGP exams, your dog must heel on your left, and it is in this position that she will receive commands to "Sit," "Down," or "Stand." When your dog can solidly execute the positions, you can also move forward by giving her commands while standing with your back to her. When doing this, however, you will need either a helper or a mirror to be sure that your dog is doing well.

Again, when she is consistently successful with your tabletop exercises, you may wish to work on only one position at a time. Or, you may wish to vary the proceedings by changing the reward from food to a ball or a tug.

The Sit Position

You may decide to teach your dog to sit while she is on leash and you have a piece of food in your right hand. Position your dog on your left side with her shoulder blade aligned with your knee. Keep the leash short so your dog cannot move away. Move your right hand up to her head, and as you do so, glide your left hand down to bring her back down. The movement of your treat-bearing hand and your gliding hand will cause your dog to sit. As soon as she sits, click or cue and then reward your dog. Repeat this several times; she should sit down as your right hand moves up and your left hand glides down.

The next step is to begin heeling in circles and then helping your dog sit. When you observe that she no longer needs your hands to guide her, attach the "Sit" command to her action. The sequence is 1. Help, command, click, reward; 2. Command, help if necessary, click, reward. When your dog understands the command and can quickly assume the right position, change the reward from food to a ball or a tug. The ball or tug will improve your dog's focus on you, and that concentration is important at the IGP exams.

When your dog understands what "Sit" requires, slowly remove all the extra help you have been giving her until all you need to do is utter the command. The next step is to teach your dog to sit and stay even as you advance forward without looking back. If you have laid a solid Sit foundation, your dog should have no trouble learning to sit and stay.

Learning to Sit in Motion

When teaching your dog the Sit in Motion exercise, give the command to sit and then turn. If she sits, stays, and continues looking up at you, wait a few seconds and then give the cue word and a reward. Progress to taking a step away from her before turning around, and so on. As always, move forward with training in small steps until you can advance at least 15 paces from your sitting dog. When you are walking away, your dog must sit calmly, concentrating on you.

If your dog becomes distracted and stops looking at you, consider surprising her. Suddenly squat, give the cue word, and allow your dog to come and get her reward. If you have been consistent in training with the cue word, your dog knows the cue word ushers in a reward. The surprise of you suddenly squatting will encourage your dog to stay focused on you. After all, this surprise was a pleasant one. Your dog would not want to miss such a surprise, should it happen again!

IGP Trial for Sit

If you have taught your dog to sit perfectly, you have made a wonderful start. For the trial, your dog will have to heel perfectly for 10 to 15 paces before you give the command to sit. While training for this, vary the number of paces you advance, otherwise your dog may start to slow down or heel behind you when she knows you are about to say "Sit." You see, many dogs like to cooperate with their handlers and are already thinking ahead! To avoid this kind of prediction on the part of your dog, make it clear that the number of steps always varies before it is time to sit. At the trial, count your paces so you are sure you are advancing between 10 and 15, rather than nine or 16. You can be sure the judge is counting, too, and deducting points if the number of paces is not correct.

Another IGP rule you should keep in mind while training is the three-second pause between when you stop after advancing away from your sitting dog and when you return to the right side of your dog. As you progress in the training, it is important to wait at least three seconds before you give the cue word and the reward, or else your dog will become restless, expecting her reward directly.

The Down Position

If you want to teach your dog the Down position separately from the other positions, try the following method that makes use of two contact points on your dog's body: one at the withers between the shoulder blades and the other at the croup between the hips. Your dog will lie down if you push gently on these two points. Keep your hand on her back when she is down and then give her a food reward. If this goes well, the next step is to wait until she makes eye contact with you before you give her the treat. After that, give her the reward the moment her body touches the ground. You can practice these exercises at home, inside or outside. Remember that training your dog to maintain eye contact with you will pay off at the IGP exam when you perform the exercise Down Under Distraction.

When your dog understands what is expected when you say "Down" and can assume the position without help, go to the training center or training field and see how she does there, amidst all the distractions. She should go down quickly, lying straight and calm, concentrating on you and making eye contact. As soon as she is down, reward her with food. As you have done with other commands, repeat the exercise at the training ground several times.

The next step is to walk backward away from your dog: you should be facing her and she should be concentrating on you. As you move backward, say, "Down," and then say the cue word and give the reward if she has done well. If your dog continues to do well as you practice this, you can progress to saying "Down" while she is heeling. Walk a few paces first before giving the command.

When you are sure your dog understands the command "Down," go to the training center and continue training her to lie down.

Remember to give the reward only if she goes down perfectly. If she is not going down perfectly, there is no reward and you should repeat the exercise. Finally, when your dog can heel at a normal speed and go down well, switch up the heeling speeds from slow to fast to normal, giving the command to go down at a variety of paces.

Recall

To teach your dog the recall part of exercise 3, Down with Recall, put some food in your hand and then bring your hands together in a V shape before standing in front of her. She should be sitting straight, settled right on the ground and close to you. Give her the food reward if she holds her position and as soon as she makes eye contact with you. When your dog understands this position, change the reward from food to the ball or tug. Only reward your dog if she is sitting perfectly. When you use a ball or a tug, make sure you throw it between your legs behind you; your dog is then allowed to run between your legs to retrieve the toy. Fun!

When she understands that she must retrieve the toy quickly and then return, train your dog to take up the basic position when she gets back to you. By this time, she should know the basic position inside and out, but at first you can help her assume the position with some food in your hand (as was described in Chapter 8).

The IGP Trial for Down with Recall

When you undergo the exam for Down with Recall, ensure you count your steps. After varying your steps during training, you want to make sure you take the necessary 10 to 15 steps at the trial so you won't lose points. Starting with the perfect basic position, move forward 10 to 15 paces with your dog at heel, and then say, "Down." You are allowed that window of five paces to choose the right moment to give the command—ensure your dog is concentrating on you when you ask her to "Down" so that she hears the command clearly and thus executes the position perfectly. Again, count your paces—there should be 30—as you move straight forward, away from your dog. If you think you might be too nervous to count, anticipate this and watch where other handlers have stopped and turned around during their exams. This will help you get a sense of how far you need to walk.

After you turn around, wait until the judge gives you the signal to call your dog. When training for this moment, wait a few seconds before calling, and during that pause don't look at your dog but at something else going on at the training center. Your dog needs to be used to you not always focusing on her. After you call your dog, finish the exercise with her in the basic position, at which point you can briefly praise her. Remember that you have to assume a new basic position before you can begin the next exercise at a trial.

The Stand Position

If you did not use a table to train your dog the Stand position, try the following method. Put your dog on leash and have her stay when her forelegs are parallel to one another. If her legs are slightly out of line, make a small movement and put your hand slightly under your dog's belly to help her stand with her front legs in line. You could also put a bar on the ground to help you keep those legs in line. As soon as the position looks good, give your dog a cue word or click and then give the reward. When she understands the position you expect from her but her stand is not quite right, allow her to correct herself before giving the reward. As soon as everything is going well consistently, add the command "Stand" to her action. When she is able to stand at your command without having to correct herself, you can move on to the next step in training your dog to stand: adding movement.

Begin by walking in a circle with your dog heeling on a leash. Only advance a few paces at first before saying "Stand," using hand movements to help your dog assume the position. If all goes well, say the cue word and offer the reward. Progress from this point by working on the position at the training center, which provides all kinds of distractions for your dog. Start by walking backward, facing your dog, before giving the command. Next, train your dog to stand while you are walking together (the dog at heel) at a variety of speeds: slow, fast, and normal. Review the methods used earlier in this chapter to train your dog to sit and lie down and apply those same ideas to training your dog to stand.

The IGP Trial for Stand While Walking

Begin this exercise as you began the Sit exercise. Again, ensure you count your paces—between 10 and 15—and choose the right moment to say "Stand." After your dog stands, begin counting your steps again, 15 paces straight ahead before you stop, turn, and wait for the judge's signal to return to your dog. Make sure you take up a good position beside your dog at the end of the exercise so that she will sit in the correct basic position after you say "Sit."

The IGP Trial for Stand While Running

Again, start with the basic position and set out, counting 10 to 15 paces, this time running with your dog at heel, before asking your dog to "Stand." It's more difficult to count your paces while running, so make sure you practice this during training. It really would be a pity to lose points at the trial for incorrect counting!

Your dog should have no problem running at heel because you will have practiced this. Make sure you command her to "Stand" when she is concentrating well, within that five-pace window after your 10th running step.

Review the recall and finish portions of this exercise in the information above on the Down exercise. During a trial, even if you are feeling nervous, try to remain calm and speak clearly. If you've trained your dog well, she will be able to successfully complete the exercises, despite your frayed nerves!

10

The Retrieving Exercises

IGP 1 has two retrieving exercises: Retrieve On the Flat and
Retrieve Over a Hurdle. IGP 2 and 3 have three retrieving exer-
cises: Retrieve On the Flat, Retrieve Over a Hurdle, and Retrieve
Over a Scaling Wall.*

Do not teach your dog to retrieve using any kind of force or
pressure. Those days are over, and a good thing, too. Instead, try
the methods we recommend below, using positive reinforcement
and a technique called Obedience Retrieve.

Retrieve with Positive Reinforcement

This first method employs positive reinforcement during play-
time: working with two toys and practicing several exercises, you
instill a love of retrieving in your dog or puppy. First, pick out two
toys, tugs, or balls on ropes. Ensure these toys are ones your dog
likes to hold in her mouth simultaneously. To begin, throw a toy
so your dog can catch it in her mouth. Pull gently on the toy when
your dog has a firm grip on it; she should try to hold on to the toy.
After a few seconds, throw the second toy for your dog to catch,

---

* IGP 1 includes the exercise Climbing over a Scaling Wall, in which the dog
sits in front of the scaling wall, and the handler goes to the other side and
calls the dog, but no retrieving is required.

even as she continues to hold the first toy. As you play with the toys, try throwing both at once. When your dog picks one up in her mouth, move the second toy by kicking it away, slowly, until she has a grip on that toy, too. Once she understands that she is to retrieve both toys, you can try throwing one toy to the left and one to the right, and then encourage her to retrieve the one on the left before picking up the one on the right. Progress from the left-right throws by throwing the first toy to the left but then keeping the other toy in your hand. Your dog will run to pick up the thrown toy, and then she will run quickly over to you so she can have the second toy. When your dog is consistently successful in practicing this exercise, consider increasing the distance of your throw. By now, retrieving is a game for your dog, not a forced behavior that decreases her speed and joy.

When your dog has matured—lost her baby teeth and gained her adult teeth—you can start working with a dumbbell. From the moment you introduce it to your dog, the dumbbell should always be treated as a tool for work, not as a toy. Your dog needs to learn to be quiet with the dumbbell, not to chew it or cause it to make noise. Judges at IGP trials deduct points if dogs chew on dumbbells or otherwise are noisy with them. To ensure your dog understands that the dumbbell is a quiet, serious tool, use a clicker and rewards and go through the following exercises. (Make sure your dog already knows what the click means: "This is an expected and desirable behavior!")

Sit in a chair with your dog in front of you, the dumbbell in your hand. Move the dumbbell a bit; keep it active and don't let it hang down. As soon as your dog shows interest in the dumbbell, click the clicker and give her a reward for being interested. Then, when your dog takes the dumbbell in her mouth, click and reward again. Your dog should have a firm grasp on the dumbbell; her mouth should be closed around it. Ensure you click and reward at the right moments. After your dog has taken it in her mouth at least 10 times correctly, change things up a bit. Click and reward after she has kept the dumbbell in her mouth calmly for different lengths of time, for example. As well, now is the time to add the command "Bring" to the exercise. When your dog takes the dumbbell firmly in her mouth and sits in front of you, ask her to "Bring" and then click or say the cue word before giving her a reward.

Once your dog understands that she must keep the dumbbell firmly and calmly in her mouth until the click sounds (or cue word is given), you can progress to working with a toy under your chin. Ask your dog—dumbbell in her mouth—to "Sit," and then take one step back and say "Bring." She should step forward—dumbbell still held quietly in her mouth—at which point you ask her to "Sit" again. Click, or say the cue word, and then drop the toy you are holding under your chin. When you hold the toy under your chin, you compel your dog to focus on your face and

Use a clicker during training to encourage your dog to hold the dumbbell quietly and calmly.

the toy, which encourages her to concentrate while holding the dumbbell.

When this toy-under-chin exercise is working out well, change things up. For example, ask your dog to lie down and then put the dumbbell behind her, wait a couple of seconds, then ask her to "Bring." As always, click and reward if she has done what you asked of her. Next, put the dumbbell in front of your lying dog, wait a second, and say, "Bring." Vary the manner in which you expect your dog to bring the dumbbell: sometimes ask her to "Bring" and "Sit" in front of you; other times, allow her to run through your legs and then sit, teaching her to move quickly and sit close to you. Command her to "Out" after she runs through your legs, and she should drop the dumbbell. Click the clicker and reward her with the ball. (You will have already taught your puppy the command "Out" when playing ball together. When your puppy first released the ball during play, you said, "Out," then clicked and rewarded her. Later, you added the command "Out" to the game when she released the ball.)

While training, make sure your dog knows all the steps that are required for a proper retrieve. Work out all the steps with the two toys to begin with, and then exchange the toys for a dumbbell and a ball. If you have laid a solid training foundation and began by playing and giving positive reinforcement, your dog will be highly motivated to do well in the retrieving exercises.

Obedience Retrieve

The second method you can use to teach your dog to retrieve is called Obedience Retrieve. Start out by teaching your dog to hold the dumbbell calmly in her mouth, using a clicker and a food treat. Have her sit in front of you as you sit in a chair with the treat (some cheese, perhaps) in your mouth and the dumbbell in your hands. As soon as your dog shows interest in the dumbbell, click and reward her by spitting a piece of cheese over to her. The next time, your dog will come closer to you and the dumbbell;

again, click and reward. Soon, your dog will take the dumbbell in her mouth, and again you should click and spit some bits of cheese over to her. By this time, your dog will understand that you want her to hold the dumbbell in her mouth until you click (or say a cue word). She also knows that a reward follows. You will probably need to repeat each of these steps between 15 and 20 times before everything runs smoothly. Then, you can add the command "Bring" to the exercise at the part where you ask your dog to take the dumbbell in her mouth. Progress from here by exchanging the cheese treat for a ball under your chin—or held in front of you under your training vest—that you drop at the end of the exercise as a reward.

The next step is for you to offer your dog the dumbbell, then take one step back. Your dog should hold the dumbbell firmly and calmly, watching you. Command, "Bring," and your dog should come quickly to offer you the dumbbell. Vary her reward, sometimes giving her cheese, sometimes a ball. When your dog understands how to perform the exercise, increase the distance you back up and vary the positions from which your dog has to grip the dumbbell. For example, have her lie down with the dumbbell in front of her. When you say, "Bring," she should pick up the dumbbell and bring it to you as quickly as she can. After that, ask her to lie down and have her pick up the dumbbell that you have positioned behind her.

Obedience Retrieve exercises may seem similar to the positive reinforcement exercises, but they do provide one distinct advantage: your dog learns to retrieve in a low drive, which makes it easier for her to take in the whole picture. She can focus on her behavior and listen to you and your commands. Learning in high motivation or drive is difficult for dogs that are highly sensitive to their surroundings. They become hysterical and cannot focus. They start acting out, barking, jumping, turning around in circles, and so on. Average or low-drive dogs will do well if you use the positive reinforcement exercises described above—they will thrive on the motivation that the two toys give them. These dogs need motivation to help them develop speed and focus while performing the exercises.

Regardless of the method you choose, as soon as the retrieving training is going well, you can start teaching your dog how to execute the retrieving exercises as they are outlined in the IGP regulations.

The IGP Trial for Retrieve On the Flat

During this exercise, your dog must retrieve a dumbbell of varying weight, depending on the IGP level:

IGP 1. 1.4 pounds (650 g)
IGP 2. 2.2 pounds (1,000 g)
IGP 3. 4.4 pounds (2,000 g).

From the basic position, you throw the dumbbell about 33 feet (10 m) away. Your off-leash dog should be sitting calmly next to you and may only set out quickly and directly to retrieve the dumbbell when the dumbbell is lying still and you have asked her to "Bring." She should set off promptly, pick the dumbbell up quickly, and return directly. Once your dog has returned, she should sit close and straight in front of you, holding the dumbbell in her mouth until you say "Out." Then, when you say "Heel," your dog must quickly take the basic position, sitting straight on your left side with her shoulder aligned with your knee. Throughout this exercise, you, the handler, may not change positions.

Changing positions is the mistake most commonly made by handlers during the Retrieve On the Flat exercise. To avoid making this mistake at the trials, remember that your training habit of moving backward to help your dog take the right position is not allowed during exams. Try to train yourself out of that habit before you register for an IGP trial.

Another thing to watch for during training is the three-second pause that must be honored before you can give the "Out" command. During training, wait at least four seconds. And always

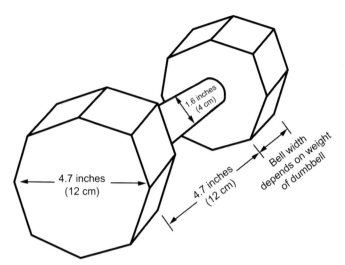

1.6 inches (4 cm)

4.7 inches (12 cm)

4.7 inches (12 cm)

Bell width depends on weight of dumbbell

During the IGP trial for retrieving exercises, you must use the dumbbell provided for you by the hosting club, not your own personal one. The dumbbell's weight must be correct for the IGP level, and the brace should be 1.5 inches (4 cm) from the ground and made of wood.

remember that being hasty as you train retrieving will only make your dog nervous and insecure, which leads to mistakes. Make sure you include every step we mention above during training, and repeat exercises until your dog is consistently successful. After all, you can earn a lot of points in the three retrieving exercises.

Jumping

For the exercises Retrieve Over a Hurdle and Retrieve Over a Scaling Wall, your dog must know how to perform a free jump and be able to climb. However, it is not good for a dog under the age of one year to jump too much because it can adversely affect the development of her hips and elbows. Wait until your dog is one year at least before beginning to train her to jump. In the meantime, you can prepare your dog for jump training by first teaching her how to recognize and approach a target, using the command "Jump." The target should be a white plastic square, eight by eight inches (20×20 cm).

As your dog ages
and develops,
increase the
distance between
the hurdle bar
and the ground.

Begin by putting the square target no more than 28 inches (70 cm) in front of your dog. Place a treat on the target and hold another treat of the same type in your hand. When everything is in position, say "Jump," and your dog will run to the target and take the treat. Call your dog to you and give her the other treat. As soon as she understands this exercise, place a plastic bar mere inches off the ground between your dog and the target. You can gradually raise this bar—up to four inches (10 cm) off the ground—as your dog experiences success in training. Jumping over something this low will not hurt your growing dog. Increase the distance between the bar and the ground as your dog ages and develops. Adding the bar to the training will help your dog understand that she must jump before she can reach the target.

In training for this exercise, you may wish to invest in a remote-controlled reward dispenser—such as the Treat & Train machine—so you do not always have to go out to the target to deposit the treat. Place the dispenser at the target and click the remote as soon as your dog is running, thereby ensuring that a treat is ready for her when she arrives. Treat gathered at the target, your dog will then race back to you, jump again, and receive her second treat from your hand.

When your dog understands what is expected and can complete a 6.5–10-foot (2–3-m) dash (including the jump) at a high speed, you can ask her to begin the exercise in the basic position before saying "Jump." A short leash comes in handy when you are teaching your dog to sit calmly and wait for "Jump." You should not pull on her leash, but hold her firmly so she cannot preempt your command and perform a false start. The leash helps, and so does your demeanor. Work quietly and your dog will understand that she, too, should be calm and wait for your command to "Jump." Only then, after all, will the treats be dispensed!

As soon as your dog understands the whole sequence of the exercise, you can increase the distance and (bearing in mind your dog's age and level of development) raise the bar. However, when you are at the point where the bar is high enough for the dog to walk beneath it, you need to either buy or build a hurdle. The hurdle should be adjustable; you should be able to make it higher or lower between 1.7 and 3.3 feet (50 and 100 cm). Consider raising the hurdle bar four inches (10 cm) every time you progress in training. This way, your dog will learn to free jump a 3.3-foot (1-m) hurdle. Note that some dogs have a problem with their hind legs as they jump, and they tip the hurdle. Such dogs need to learn to jump higher so their hind quarters clear the hurdle every time. You can use a training tool—the JumpControlTrainer, for example—or a bar with brushes on the hurdle to encourage your dog to jump higher.

When you are training your dog to free jump a 3.3-foot (1-m) hurdle, continue to place the target on the other side of the jump. Once your dog is successfully jumping the hurdle and solidly retrieving on the flat, put the parts of the exercise together. When you do this, the hurdle should be about 1.7 feet (50 cm) high; again, increase the height as the dog masters each level, increasing to 3.3 feet (1 m) when your dog has no problem with the exercise.

Some dogs have trouble clearing their hind legs when they jump a hurdle, invariably tipping the hurdle when they jump. One way to help your dog to learn to jump higher and thus secure a free jump is to use a training aid like the JumpControlTrainer, invented by Markus Mohr. This contraption's key piece is a section of fishing line—invisible to the dog—fixed taut above the hurdle. If the dog touches the line when jumping the hurdle, the aid emits a tone that frightens the dog and reminds her to jump higher.

As you work, figure out what distance between you and your dog and the hurdle gives your dog the best chance to execute a fine free jump. Also, find out what distance is best between the hurdle and where the dumbbell lands—you have to be able to comfortably throw the dumbbell to that point, and your dog has to be comfortable with that distance, too. Once you have figured everything out, you can start practicing this exercise as it is outlined in the IGP regulations.

The IGP Trial for Retrieve Over a Hurdle

At the trial, stand with your off-leash dog in the basic position, a minimum of 13.1 feet (4 m) in front of the 3.3-foot (1-m) hurdle. Throw the 1.4-pound (650-g) dumbbell over the hurdle. Your dog should sit calmly next to you, waiting attentively for you to say, "Jump." Then, she must set off quickly and directly. As she is

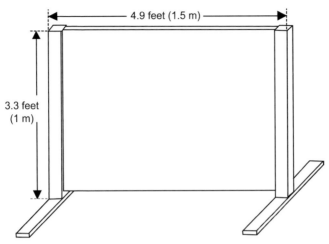

4.9 feet (1.5 m)

3.3 feet
(1 m)

The IGP-regulation hurdle has a height of 3.3 feet (1 m) and a width of
4.9 feet (1.5 m).

jumping the hurdle, command, "Bring." After the free jump, your
dog should run directly to the dumbbell, pick it up immediately,
turn, run, and jump back over the hurdle. When she reaches you,
she must sit close in front of you, holding the dumbbell calmly
until after three seconds you say, "Out," at which point your dog
should present the dumbbell to you. Say, "Heel," and your dog
should assume the basic position quickly. Remember, you should
not change your position during the exercise.

Note that if you throw the dumbbell too far to one side, or if
the dumbbell lands in such a way that it is difficult for the dog to
see it, you may ask for a re-throw. If the judge grants your request,
your dog must remain sitting as you retrieve the dumbbell. It is not
always possible for you to see that you have thrown the dumbbell
too far to one side or into an otherwise bad position.

A lot of training centers have fences around the hurdles so the
dog is compelled to jump back over the hurdle to return to her
handler. However, the shape of these fences can be an issue. To
be effective, the fence should be placed in a half-circle extending
from either side of the hurdle. This way, even if you throw the

When training your dog to retrieve the dumbbell over the hurdle, consider adding a fence that extends at least 10 feet (3 m) out from the hurdle on both sides. This fence will ensure that your dog jumps back over the hurdle after retrieving, even if the dumbbell is thrown a yard or so to the left or right.

dumbbell a bit to the left or right of the hurdle (but still in the fenced area), the dog learns she must always jump the hurdle again to bring the dumbbell back to you. The half-circle fence prevents your dog from skirting the hurdle on her return to you.

Climbing a Scaling Wall

The last of the retrieve exercises involves your dog climbing a scaling wall, which is not as difficult to train for as the free jump over the 3.3-foot (1-m) hurdle. Before you begin, ensure you have access to a scaling wall that you can adjust to a very low height. Take two plastic pipes and bend them into half-circles. Affix one pipe on the left side and one on the right, with one end of the pipe fixed to the front and the other end fixed to the back of the scaling wall to stop your dog from trying to jump directly to the top of the wall and then jump off the top. The plastic pipes will stop her from jumping, making sure your dog does not injure herself and instead learns to scramble up and down the wall. Once the half-circle pipes are in place, put the white plastic square target you used in hurdle training on the other side of this wall, and you are ready to begin.

Dogs usually find the scaling wall easier to master than the 3.3-foot (1-m) hurdle.

As she did during hurdle training, your dog receives two treats when she trains for this exercise: one at the target and then one from you. In the beginning, let her climb up and down, forward and back, several times, until she understands how to negotiate the wall. Then, you can raise the wall up a bit, increasing its height with consistent successes until the wall is 70.9-inch (180 cm) tall, as is prescribed in the IGP regulations. As soon as your dog is able to climb up and down without a problem or hesitation, start to ask her to retrieve over the wall adjusted to a low height. Only do this if your dog is already able to successfully retrieve on the flat.

You may decide to put a fence up by the sides of the wall so that your dog isn't able to circle around the wall instead of climbing it to return to you. Such a fence prevents your dog from forming the bad habit of going around the wall, so you will not have to worry about her doing this at a trial. In IGP 1 only climbing the scaling wall is required.

The IGP 2 or 3 Trials for Retrieve Over a Scaling Wall

Begin the exercise by standing with your dog in the basic position at a minimum of 13.1 feet (4 m) in front of the 70.9-inch (180-cm) -high scaling wall. Your off-leash dog should sit calmly as you throw the dumbbell over the wall. When you command, "Jump," your dog should run to the scaling wall, and as she climbs over the wall, ask her to "Bring." Your dog should run directly to the dumbbell, pick it up immediately, and then run back to the scaling wall, which she again climbs in order to return to you. When she arrives, your dog must sit close in front of you and hold the dumbbell calmly in her mouth, waiting to present it to you when you command, "Out," about three seconds after she has sat down. When you have the dumbbell in hand, ask your dog to "Heel," and she should assume the correct basic position.

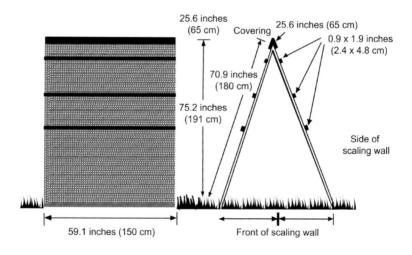

The scaling wall consists of two sides—59.1 inches (150 cm) wide and 75.2 inches (191 cm) high— joined at the top. The bottom of the two sides should rest on the ground so that the wall is a horizontal height of 70.9 inches (180 cm). The entire area of the scaling wall, including the top angle, must be covered with anti-skid material. The upper portion of each side should have three climbing slats measuring 0.9 by 1.9 inches (2.4 x 4.8 cm) each.

Make sure you do not change your position during the exercise. Note, again, that if your throw is wide or if the dumbbell lands in an inaccessible location, you may ask for a re-throw. If the judge grants you a re-throw, your dog has to remain seated while you retrieve the dumbbell.

In this retrieving exercise, the same things are important at the trial as those in the other two retrieving exercises. As well, dog handlers should understand the regulations and present the exercises as they are written. Whether or not you are able to execute the exercises perfectly depends on what happened in your training sessions. Remember that during training it always helps for you to ask a colleague to watch you and your dog go through the exercises and then give you feedback about mistakes, what you've done well, and possibly provide advice on how to improve.

11

Send Out and Down Under Distraction

The last exercise in the obedience part of all levels of IGP is Send Out with Down, which is not an easy exercise. You, the handler, must train the two parts of this exercise separately. First, train your dog the Down at a distance and then the Send Out in full speed. This Send Out with Down exercise must be presented at full speed during the trials; your dog must move quickly and lie down quickly, which at first training may be awkward for the dog.

There are several methods to teach this exercise to a dog; choose your method with your dog's temperament in mind.

When performing the Send Out with Down exercise, your dog must run away from you at full speed and then lie down in one motion when commanded.

Using the Bite-training Pillow

This first method employs high motivation to develop high speed. Use a flat bite-training pillow that has three handles. Ask a helper to take the bite pillow to a ditch—your dog should be watching the helper do this. Then, send your dog out to retrieve the pillow—your helper and dog should play with the pillow, tugging and pulling, as they come back to you. After a few repeats of this exercise, your dog will not need to see the helper go into the ditch to know that on your command she must run the entire distance to where she knows she will find that person with the pillow. Later, the helper can put the pillow down in the ditch and leave; your dog will know that she must find the pillow and bring it back to you quickly.

After your dog, the helper, and you have played with the pillow in the above exercise for some time, start taking the high-motivation action out of the bite-pillow training, first employing short distances. So, ask the dog to lie down after walking a few paces together. As soon as she does, say a cue word and allow her to take the pillow and play with it. In the next training sessions, extend the distance you advance together and the amount of time your dog has to lie down to receive her reward. This variety of distances and length of time spent lying down is important—again, your dog should not become used to a particular routine with the Down exercise.

If your dog is able to successfully complete all of the above exercises consistently, you can begin to put the two parts of the exercise together. Position yourself about a yard (1 m) from the ditch, send your dog out, and command, "Down." If your dog goes down, speak the cue word and then kneel and let your dog catch the pillow and play with it and you. Your dog must understand clearly that she only gets to play with the pillow after she has gone down quickly and correctly in response to you saying "Down." Sometimes your dog should race to the pillow;

sometimes you should hold the pillow when you send your dog out. If the pillow is not in front of your dog, you must make it clear that she will still get to play with the pillow after going down. You do this by kneeling and clicking or giving the cue word before your dog is allowed to come to you and to play. Remember that it is important for you to kneel before allowing your dog to come and play with the pillow. This action must not be enacted at the trial, where your dog will have to work without a reward. Still, your dog will stay focused on you, watch to see if you will kneel, and know what is expected of her before she can reap her reward or will stay down until you come to her and command her to assume the basic position.

As you progress in training for this exercise, increase the distance your dog must run until she is running at least 33 yards (30 m), the distance she will have to run at the trial. Also during training, send your dog out in different directions so she understands that the exercise can be performed in different ways.

Training with Food or a Ball

The bite-pillow method works well for dogs that do not have a problem training in a high drive. However, for the dogs that learn better in a lower drive, you can teach this exercise using food or a ball as incentive. Again, teach your dog the Send Out and the Down separately but during the same time period.

To teach your dog to go down, ensure you have a target, preferably a blue plastic square that is about eight by eight inches (20×20 cm). The best colors for targets are white and blue because they stand out on green grass. Do not use white, though, because you have already used a white target when teaching your dog to jump.

Teach your dog to go down quickly when she reaches the blue target. Throw a piece of cheese or a treat between five to eight yards (4–5 m) away from where you are standing. While your dog goes to pick up the treat, put the blue target down on the ground

Teach your dog how to lie down and then send out separately but in succession. When teaching your dog to lie down, we recommend that you use a blue, plastic, square target measuring eight by eight inches (20x20 cm).

and palm another treat, then crouch down beside the target, placing your hand with the treat in the down-signal position over the target. When she returns, she will know what you expect because your dog already knows (from the table work) that she has to lie down. After she is down, click and reward her with the treat. Release your dog from lying down by saying the cue word, and then throw another treat out for her to fetch. Repeat this exercise several times and you will see that your dog understands that she has to lie down on the blue target. As you repeat the exercise, slowly bring your hand up higher, and then stand up. As soon as your dog is down, reward her with food, giving her pieces of food for as long as you want her to lie down in that session. Then, speak the cue word and your dog will get ready to go again. Vary the position of the target, but follow the same procedure until your dog goes down quickly at the target without any hesitation after you say, "Down."

The next step in training has your dog learning how to lie down some distance from you. Stand with your dog about 20 inches (50 cm) from the target. Make sure you've already placed a treat on the target. Send your dog out to the target and give the command "Down." Increase the distance between you and the target with consistent success. If all is going well at a distance of a yard (1 m) from the target, you may begin to switch the reward from food to a ball or other toy.

When you are ready, go with your dog to the end of the training field, position the target, and place a ball on it. Then, lead your dog to about a yard's distance from the target and send her over to the target to pick up the ball. Repeat this as long as is necessary, until your dog knows she is allowed to pick up the ball. Increase your distance from the target, and your dog will begin to understand that she must run quickly to pick up the ball. Every now and then, this exercise can be trained over the whole length of the field because it helps your dog associate speed with the Send Out exercise. The command associated with this exercise is "Go out," which can be added to the exercise as soon as you notice that your dog understands what is expected of her.

When your dog understands that she must go down for food on the target, and that she can pick up her ball during the send out, you can start making the target smaller. Again, variety during training is essential: sometimes use food and sometimes use the ball. As the target decreases in size, commands for the Send Out and the Down remain the same. It is not only important to vary the exercise in terms of the ball and treat, but also to practice the exercise in different places, sending out in different directions and amidst different outside stimuli.

By the end of training, you will have reduced the target to nothing, but your dog will know what to do when you command her to "Go out" and "Down." Speed is important on the send out; steadiness and immediacy are important on the down. If everything is in place, you can begin working on presenting Send Out with Down for the trial.

Consider using a ball machine when training to encourage your dog to send out as quickly as possible.

The IGP Trial for Send Out with Down

Start training for the trial with a correct basic position followed by 10 to 15 steps of heeling before you say, "Go out." You will likely find that your dog likes to be sent out, and so she might heel too far in front of you. To avoid this problem, make a variety of turns as you step forward; never advance the 10 to 15 steps in a straight line when you are training. As well, keep your dog on her toes by varying the number of steps you take before you send her out. You must take at least 10 steps, but start with more than that; otherwise, your dog will begin to know what is going on and will be ready to run on the 11th step. Again with our refrain: variety in training is the key to success!

When at the trial, your command "Down," must be given at the judge's instructions. You may wish to train for this at the training center, asking a colleague to play the judge. This way, you get used to paying attention to somebody beside or behind you, even as you concentrate on your dog. Your dog will also become used to you not focusing totally on her and will therefore not be thrown off at the trial when you have to pay attention to the judge.

You must be ready to act on the judge's instruction to ask your dog to rise from her down position. When training for this, always wait a few seconds beside your dog before you say, "Sit." If your dog tends to rise without a command, have her go down again and then wait a few seconds before giving the "Sit" command. She needs to know that she has to wait for you to say "Sit" before she can rise. Train all of these difficulties away on the training field, and you will not have a problem at the trial.

Down Under Distraction

The first or the last exercise in Phase B of IGP trials is Down Under Distraction, often called the Long Down. It is not the most difficult exercise in the program, but as the handler, you must have a lot of patience and be able to train your dog consistently leading up to the trials. The exercise has three parts: heeling to the indicated place, lying down under distraction, and getting up again. In former chapters, we have suggested how to train your dog to heel perfectly (see page 89), as well as the Down position (see page 106). For this exercise, your dog must stay down for a long time, despite many distractions, and with her handler far away and with her back to the dog. The exercise is truly a test of the dog's concentration and your ability on the training field.

When you begin to train for this exercise, consider using a stopwatch to see how long your dog is already able to stay lying down and focused. Start by having your dog lie down for a minute when you are standing a couple of yards (2 m) away from her. Don't allow your dog to change positions by, for instance, lying on her side or sniffing the surface of the field around her. Your dog must lie quietly, focused only on you. After the minute has elapsed, go back to your dog and give her a treat while she is lying down and staying. Then, go away again, and after 30 seconds return, stand beside your dog, and command, "Sit," allowing her to rise to basic position. After three seconds, give the cue word you have devised or click and reward your dog with food. Do not use a tug or a ball as a reward when you practice this exercise because those toys will bring your dog into a high drive, which may cause her to become antsy the next time you ask her to "Sit."

As you train for this exercise, make a schedule of time and distance. Work consistently with a stopwatch so you know how long your dog stays down during each session. When your dog is consistently steady in the Down position, start standing partly turned away from her so that she gets used to you looking away. Use a mirror to monitor how your dog is doing when you are turned away, or ask a colleague to watch your dog and immediately let you know if something has gone awry.

Many handlers are not consistent in their training of this exercise. Instead of taking the exercise seriously and paying close attention to their dogs in the Long Down, they talk to others at the training center or busy themselves with other things while their dogs lie down and wait for them. It is best to begin the training at home, even in your house. Remember to stay focused on your dog for the duration of the training session, and let your dog know how well she is doing by rewarding her work when it is going well.

If you are able to perform the exercise at home for about 15 minutes without a problem and without loss of concentration on your part or that of your dog, you are ready to train the exercise at the training center, which is replete with distractions. Both you and your dog need to be able to work through the exercise despite the environment around you: other dogs, other people, machines, and so on. As well, remember that your dog needs to be able to stay down when she hears gunfire. When you first start training at the training field, the distance between you and your dog should be short. Increase that distance and change the position of your body until you are standing a fair distance from your dog with your back to her. At a great distance, you will need someone who will watch your dog and let you know if she is losing focus. If all is going well, you can start to prepare for the trial.

The IGP Trial for Down Under Distraction

While you are training to present this exercise at a trial, ask someone to play the role of the judge. First off, this person tells you where to go with your dog. Start out directly, correctly heeling, and then make 90° turns to arrive at the place where you will put your dog into the Long Down. When you arrive at the spot, take up the basic position and look to the "judge." When the "judge" tells you to give the command, say, "Down," and your dog should go down directly. Be sure to train this on a training field or at a training center, because at this point in the exercise your focus is not completely on the dog—you are waiting for the instructions from the judge—and some dogs will sense this and go down without their handler's command because they know what is coming. If this happens to you when you are training, train this tendency out of your dog, ensuring she knows that she must wait for your command before going down. Let your dog know that you don't like it when she lies down without your command. Repeat the exercise and only reward her if she stays in the sitting position. Then, take your dog away from the place where you are training, make a turn, and go back to the start of the exercise. In this way, you vary the training so your dog learns she must wait for your commands.

After you say, "Down," do not walk away too quickly. Take your time because your dog is not yet lying steady and if you rush away, you run the risk of your dog being unquiet from the beginning. Your dog has to stay calmly in the Long Down for at least 15 minutes during training. During a trial, the Long Down exercise usually takes 10 minutes, but you never know. Something might happen during the other dog's exercises, and your dog will have to stay down longer. As well, make sure you train your dog amidst a variety of distractions, as well as the sound of guns firing. If you train your dog in this way, she should be used to staying down for a long time amidst many distractions, and she should stay down and calm during the trial.

During a trial, the judge will give you a sign that you can ask your dog to rise. While training, when the Long Down is over, stand next to your dog and then wait at least three seconds, sometimes longer, before saying "Sit." Take care that you are standing in the right place so that your dog will be in the correct basic position after sitting up on command. If you have trained your dog well through all the steps of this exercise, you won't have a problem during the IGP trial.

Phase C

Protection

12

Protection Work Basics

In IGP's Protection phase (Phase C), you and your dog work
together to perform several exercises designed to test your dog's
courage, power, and control. During this phase, the training field
is equipped with several blinds in which a helper, also called a
decoy, can hide. You direct your dog to search the blinds for the
decoy. When he finds the decoy, he barks. Your dog must guard the
decoy to prevent him from moving until you recall your dog. After
this, the decoy attempts to "escape"; your dog must prevent this by
biting the padded sleeve on the decoy's arm. Other exercises in this
phase include Defense Against an Attack and the Back Transport
or Side Transport.

When the decoy stops the attack or escape, your dog has to release
his sleeve. You may give the command "Out," but you have to give
that command while standing calmly and not influencing your dog.
After the release, your dog is to remain close to the decoy and watch
him attentively. If your dog does not release the sleeve after the first
permitted command, the judge will instruct you to command, "Out,"
again. If he still does not release the sleeve after the third command,
your dog will be labeled "Out of Control" and disqualified.

During this phase at the trials, the judge evaluates your dog's
bite according to depth and fullness of grip. Also, your dog must

demonstrate power, commitment, courage, attentive and focused intensity during the guarding, strong and firm grips, and an active fight against the decoy in each exercise, always remaining under your verbal control. Obedience and control are essential in this phase. A stable and secure dog, not a vicious dog, is required for this work. Your dog must show the courage to engage the decoy and the temperament to obey you, the handler, while in a high drive. Your dog must show enthusiasm in his work, because the judge will dismiss a dog that shows fear, lack of control, or inappropriate aggression.

Mistakes in the Buildup to Training

As we've suggested throughout this book, a good relationship between you and your dog is one of the keys to successful training. Your dog should respect your authority but also enjoy working with you. The bond you have with your dog as you embark on protection training should be especially strong. If your relationship with your dog is not optimal, you can bet you will encounter problems with obedience, and the protection exercises will become a source of frustration for both you and your dog. Before beginning protection work, ensure that your dog always listens and responds to your commands.

As well, before you begin training for this phase, it is also crucial that your dog is able to physically and mentally handle everything that goes with the biting exercises that are part of protection work. He should have good, strong, adult teeth. Make sure your dog is old enough to work out the protection exercises, not only for the sake of his teeth, but also for the sake of his mental health. Dogs that are introduced to protection training at a young age often show fear when they get older, and their behavior often gets out of hand. They can either become afraid of or aggressive toward people or even become fear-biters. It is simply irresponsible to train dogs younger than a year old for protection work.

It is crucial that your dog is both mentally and physically able to handle everything that happens during protection training.

Whenever anyone discusses Schutzhund training, the protection phase is the subject that kicks up the most dust, not only among outsiders—who often think bite work is dangerous—but even among trainers, for whom dog training is central to their interests. We would like to invite those who are not part of dog-training circles to come and have a look at IGP training fields and see how trustworthy protection-trained dogs are, even as they work on protection exercises.

Trainers have a special interest in Phase C of IGP training because a dog's value is measured by his bite work. A dog that performs perfectly in tracking and obedience but does not want to bite is a big zero, according to some trainers. However, a dog's shortcomings in protection work—not biting or biting badly—and thus his devaluation, are usually because of humans and their errors: a trainer who has incorrectly built up protection-work training; an instructor who doesn't understand his profession; an unskilled decoy; or a handler who makes serious mistakes, such as not providing the necessary contact with his dog and/or who wants to make progress too quickly. Because there is so much value attached to protection, a lot of handlers set out to prove that their dogs are very good at it. They start the bite work too early, or they want to progress so quickly that they make mistakes.

Often handlers show up at training groups because their dogs are a problem at home or on the street. These dogs were not educated correctly in the beginning and as a result have behavioral problems. Handlers who bring such dogs to IGP training groups have somehow decided that now is the time to "teach" their dogs a thing or two. Many of these people think their dogs are good at biting, and so they think they must act quickly and train their dogs for protection work before they lose their ability. This kind of nonsense is not strange to the ears of experienced handlers. Still, too often, these handlers come to training centers to show off their dogs' abilities. For now, however, let us leave such individuals behind and turn ourselves to the correct methods of building up your dog's protection skills.

As with the other phases of IGP training, but perhaps more so here, you must correctly assess your dog's character before you begin protection training. Bite work training must be adjusted for each individual dog, and there is no one right package for every dog. It is also impossible to learn how to train bite work from a book, without supporting your dog. Only an experienced instructor and a skilled decoy are able to teach a dog the fine details of this phase in IGP training. From behind our desk, as we write this book, we can only give you the general rules; you and your dog must learn how to work out the intricacies from the people with the skills on the training fields.

A Passion for the Chase

First, a word about the chase passion. During agitation—or the decoy's teasing of the dog—your dog has to be focused constantly on the decoy. The decoy must, by his stance, show your dog that although he is challenging him, he is also afraid. Your dog will learn that the decoy is not really a great threat, that he can actually catch the fearful guy very easily. He has to learn that he will always win in his tussles with the decoy, and that he may even get the tug or sleeve as a prey trophy. By walking away from your dog, the decoy stimulates your dog's passion for the chase; and when your dog takes the sleeve or tug from the decoy, he satisfies his prey drive. Moving objects attract the most attention from animals. An enemy (in our case, the decoy) who takes flight from a dog stimulates that dog's passion for the chase. The dog just has to chase the decoy, whether he wants to or not.

Flight and Defensive Reactions

The handler, instructor, and decoy should know about chase passion and prey drive, but they must also know about the flight reactions of animals. Animals not only take flight in situations in which their lives are threatened, but also in many other situations. Every animal has its own reasons to take flight, and practically all wild animals, almost everywhere in the world, flee from humans (some more quickly than others). They have learned to see us as dangerous.

Dogs have learned to live closely with humans and normally are not afraid of us. That changes, however, when humans threaten them. When a human, by attitude, gestures, and words, threatens a dog and walks toward him, a dog with a weak character will flee as soon as that human reaches a certain distance from him. This distance is called the flight distance, and it is the distance at which, under threat, a dog knows he can still take flight. An animal in flight will, if the distance between him and the threat continues to decrease, take action to defend himself. The animal will threaten: show teeth, growl, and so on, all visible defense reactions meant as final warnings to the one who is threatening. If the threatening presence continues to advance, the animal will attack. The distance at which a pursued animal changes his behavior from a flight reaction to a defensive one is called the defense distance or critical distance. Just like the flight distance, the defense distance also depends on a lot of influences. The difference between the flight and defense distances is that with the defense distance, the

A Schutzhund should have a strong character and be able to take on mental pressure. Protection dogs must have a good deal of courage and toughness in order to resist threats.

animal feels seriously pushed to flee farther and knows he must attack to escape.

When threatened, dogs with weak character will try to flee from the decoy. If the decoy were then to pursue that fleeing dog and catch up with him, approaching the defensive distance, that dog should attack out of anxiety and bite out of fear. Biting out of fear can be seen as an attempt to make the way free to flee in the opposite direction. The defensive distance differs by age, breed, and individual dog.

If a decoy threatens a young dog, he will react by fleeing. We must avoid this, because when a dog begins to bite out of fear, he is unable to do his work as a Schutzhund. Protection work requires dogs with strong character that can take a lot of mental pressure and have enough courage and toughness to resist threats. Only adult dogs are strong enough to show these characteristics, so don't start agitating or teasing young dogs. As we already noted, training a dog for protection work too young can make him fearful.

Defensive Drive-Hunting Drive-Prey Drive

At the beginning of protection training, slowly get your dog used to threatening situations. It is not hard for a decoy to chase away a dog that is new to the work; it is, however, much more difficult to build courage and strength of character in a weaker dog so that he can take on bite work. The first order of business in the training, therefore, is to stimulate your dog's defensive drive, or his willingness to protect threatened pack mates (in your case, you or a member of your family) and defend them when necessary. When this drive is stimulated, a dog will resist the decoy's threats without hesitation and defend himself and his handler.

Some dogs have a stronger defensive drive than others. Because dogs have been selectively bred for beauty for so many years, today, even among working-dog breeds, many dogs have weak characters that are lacking or have a diminished natural, defensive drive. Just because your dog has a diminished defensive drive, however, does not mean he is unfit for bite work; humans have, as ever, discovered something to solve this problem. Instead of stimulating the defensive drive in weaker dogs, we stimulate their prey drive so they will engage in protection work. The prey drive is very similar to the hunting drive, which is the dog's natural drive to smell for game or to search and chase on sight.

This hunting drive goes back to the forefathers of our dogs, wolves, and finds its origins in the pressure to find food. The hunting drive is still present in our modern dogs in a more or less emphatic form, although it is no longer associated with feelings of hunger or the pressure to acquire food. So, the hunting drive is not only present in hunting dogs, but also in just about every other dog.

As noted, the prey drive is very similar to the hunting drive. Originally, a dog's prey drive grew out of the need not only to hunt game but also to catch and kill it to satisfy his hunger and that of his young. This drive is also present in many domestic dogs; however, under the influence of the play drive, it is now much more focused on chasing and demolishing toys. The skill of chasing game is now only taught to hunting dogs, so dogs now express their prey drive by chasing, catching, and shaking articles to "death."

By stimulating your dog's prey drive, you can teach him to chase a decoy that has the "prey": the bite sleeve or the tug. Then, as your dog begins to understand that he will always win the fight with the decoy, his defensive drive will kick in, and he will work up enough self-confidence and courage to bite the tug or sleeve. Every time he works with the decoy, your dog will "capture" the prey (i.e., the decoy's sleeve).

Reaction Assessment

Before beginning actual bite work, assess what your dog's reactions are to the sleeve and the decoy, and then build your training trajectory based on what you find out. Even when a dog demonstrates more than enough defensive drive in everyday situations, a good overall assessment is necessary before starting to train. For dogs with a reasonable defensive drive, the sleeve as prey is not especially interesting. Instead, these dogs focus on chasing the threatening decoy away by biting. It normally does not matter to these dogs where they bite the decoy: the first thing their snouts reach will be bitten. However, we want protection-work dogs to bite the sleeve, so we have to teach them that. This is where the decoy's ability to train with the sleeve is paramount. If these dogs learn to bite the sleeve, they will do so at the training center and elsewhere, although there are exceptions. When the dog has bitten the sleeve, the decoy should draw the sleeve up to chest height, and the handler should teach his dog to release on "Out."

This dog is focused on the decoy and will guard him correctly after releasing the sleeve.

Mental Characteristics

Defensive drive is not the only characteristic you should assess when considering a dog for IGP protection work. Only physically and mentally healthy dogs can undergo the heavy training that is involved in this kind of work. We want potential Schutzhunds to have intelligence, strength of character, a good temperament, composure, reliability, toughness, medium sharpness, and courage.

Besides that, we demand of the ideal Schutzhund some other characteristics, like devotion to his handler and family, and a willingness to work. A dog you have to wake up before going to work is not right for this kind of training! A dog that likes to work makes a lot of noise and shows a lot of interest when he sees that you are getting ready to go. As well, your dog should show both before and during work an almost tireless willingness to work. To be able to do this, your dog must be in very good physical health and have a great deal of stamina. In short, a potential Schutzhund is a dog in which you can see a clear desire to work and that needs no encouragement to continue and concentrate on his work.

INTELLIGENCE

The most important mental characteristic a dog must have for protection work is intelligence: instinctive and practical. By instinctive intelligence, we mean all hereditary skills and behavior.

For instance, every pup runs after a moving object, showing an instinctive hunting drive. By practical intelligence we mean the speed with which, and the degree to which, the dog conforms to the desires of the handler: how quickly and how correctly the dog learns the different exercises.

STRENGTH OF CHARACTER

A dog has a strong character if he behaves self-confidently, free of nervousness, fear, or jumpiness. Sudden and unexpected provocation, such as gunfire, traffic, or waving flags, do not knock him off balance.

TEMPERAMENT

A dog's temperament is expressed in his mental skills and the degree of his reaction to different provocations from the environment. The more lively a dog is and the more intensive his response to the surroundings, the higher the temperament he has. If your dog is slow in his movements and lackadaisical in response to the environment, his temperament is considered low. In the strong presence of certain drives (for instance, the guard drive), high-temperament dogs will focus intently when an appropriate and yet small ripple happens in his environment (for instance, a person approaching from far away). For IGP protection training, a high temperament is preferred. Protection dogs should be happy and attentive to training, always interested in staying active.

It is important to recognize the difference between a high-temperament dog and a nervous dog. Some people want dogs that itch to react when something happens, saying that such dogs necessarily have high temperament. This kind of reaction is three-quarters nervousness combined with a big part of sharpness (see page 150).

COMPOSURE

A Schutzhund must stay calm and show self-confidence even when placed in totally strange circumstances. He must quietly regard the situation, neither afraid nor ranting and raving, regardless of whether he finds himself among a group of people, on a deserted street, or in traffic. When a dog has composure, he is able to act the right way in the right moment.

RELIABILITY

A Schutzhund's behavior must be reliable; there should be no surprises. Protection-work dogs should not suddenly lunge at playing children or at adults, or display aggression toward housemates or to you, the handler.

Dogs that are too independent and "resist" are disturbing in everyday life, and they are not favorites for training, either. On the other end of the spectrum, a dog that is "everybody's friend" is also not always the best working dog. The right dog for Schutzhund training is one that is a bit reserved with an appropriate, medium sharpness (again, see page 150), as long as he is absolutely reliable. He must know to assess the situations he finds himself in and to act only on the command of his handler.

TOUGHNESS

In this context, toughness (or low sensitivity) means the ability to suffer unpleasant events—pain, punishment, or defeat in a fight—without being deterred and being able to forget the unpleasantness ever happened. A tough dog will not allow pain to prevent him from carrying out your commands. He will not be daunted by an attack—by a decoy, for instance—nor will he be upset by a decoy's yelling or touches with the soft stick.

Softness (or high sensitivity) is the opposite of toughness. A soft dog is strongly affected by unpleasant events or by frightening circumstances, and if he has once experienced a bad situation, he will seek to avoid a similar situation in the future. Softness must not, however, be confused with fear of pain. Some dogs are very sensitive to pain and squeal at the lightest pinch, such as an injection. However, such dogs will not necessarily lose their confidence against the one who causes the pain, in this case, the vet. Fear of pain will not necessarily influence the dog's willingness to work, because during protection work training, the dog doesn't pay attention to pain.

SHARPNESS AND COURAGE

A dog's level of sharpness determines how he reacts to unexpected events; self-preservation plays a role here. A dog whose sharpness is overdeveloped, and also lacks courage, tends to bite out of fear. Courage is connected to sharpness, in that it also involves self-preservation. A dog is considered courageous if he steps into a dangerous situation without pressure from the outside and stays in the situation: that act goes against his instinct for self-preservation.

Courage and sharpness complement one another sometimes, but they can also be opposites. The basic characteristic of a sharp dog is his hostile attitude toward the unknown, which can be based as much on self-assurance and an inherent fighting spirit as on uncertainty, distrust, and fear. In the first case, sharpness is a hereditary, natural sharpness; in the second, it is a fake sharpness acquired by training and from a need for self-defense. Regardless, the stronger the dog's drive for self-preservation, the greater his sharpness will be. The drive for self-preservation plays an opposite role in a courageous dog—one that of his own volition stays in dangerous situations.

When assessing dogs' characters, we often group courage and sharpness together in four different types: 1. Courageous–Sharp, 2. Courageous–Not Sharp, 3. Not Courageous–Sharp, and 4. Not Courageous–Not Sharp. We can describe these types as follows:

1. **Courageous–Sharp**

    The dog moves in the direction of what he sees as a danger in a hostile manner: high tail, barking or with a combative open mouth, and bristled back hairs. The dog is both fearless and combative.

2. **Courageous–Not Sharp**

    The dog is not combative, but he is indifferent or curious and does not display signs of fear. He either approaches the unusual with an interested, wagging tail, or, uninterested, continues his pursuits. This dog is fearless without hostility.

3. Not Courageous–Sharp

   This dog expresses anxious willingness to defend himself
   with bristled back hairs; usually with a hanging—but
   sometimes high—tail; and also usually growling, showing
   teeth, or barking. In such a posture and displaying such
   behavior, he withdraws from danger. He expresses anxiety
   and hostility.

4. Not Courageous–Not Sharp

   Presented with a dangerous situation, this dog is
   anxious and ready to flee, but does not show any sign
   of defending himself; he lacks a hostile attitude. He
   withdraws, tail pulled between his legs, sometimes with
   a crouched body or a crooked back, in extreme cases
   screaming with fear or urinating. This dog is anxious
   without hostility.

Suitability

Sometimes both characteristics, courage and sharpness, are mis-
takenly thought to be present in a dog but are not and therefore
training results are disappointing. In such cases, you may desire to
make such "not courageous–sharp" dogs sharper. However, under
all circumstances, an artificial increase of sharpness does not work:
training will not help the dog distinguish between acting and seri-
ousness or between apparent and real danger.

In our experience, training dogs that fall under types 3 or 4
always results in disappointment, and it does not take long before
you must stop training. It is in your best interests, and in those of
your dog, to assess character correctly and exclude inappropriate
dogs from IGP training.

A reliable Schutzhund must have a great basic confidence in
humans, and in himself. The ideal dog for this training is one that
is well-balanced, reliable, self-confident, tough, and courageous
and who also has an adapted, natural sharpness. Dogs that are
not well-balanced, not self-confident, not courageous, or too sharp
will normally fail in protection training.

A reliable Schutzhund
must have confidence
in humans and himself.

Character Traits

Many of the breeds used in IGP training are herding dogs, cattle dogs, or working dogs, which were originally bred for many different purposes. The characters and behaviors of these breeds show clear differences from other dogs, characteristics and behaviors that are preferred in Schutzhund training. We know IGP-trained dogs that were originally cattle dogs, guarding herds of cattle and escorting them independently to various locations. Such dogs include Rottweilers and Bouvier des Flandres, for instance. Other IGP-trained dogs include shepherd dogs, which originally tended flocks of sheep; on the instructions of the shepherd, these dogs kept the sheep together and moved them in the determined direction. In this group we include, among others, the German, Belgian, and Dutch shepherd dogs.

Most cattle dogs are a bit tougher to handle than shepherd dogs, and they have, in our experience, less inclination to spontaneous cooperation with the handler. This is because cattle dogs were bred to work independently, with big animals. These dogs therefore still exhibit an independent character. If one wants to train a cattle dog, he will, in the beginning, be a bit more difficult to work out than a shepherd dog. A cattle dog is often not as easy to motivate for certain exercises, and if you ever overtrain an exercise with a cattle dog, you usually end up with a dog that refuses to work anymore.

Even though it often takes longer to teach cattle dogs to perform certain exercises quickly and happily, in comparison to shepherd dogs, we have seen many Bouviers and Rottweilers that are excellent workers. And, we have found that once a cattle dog reaches a high level in IGP training, he remembers what he has been taught better than a shepherd dog and often works out the instructions more promptly, even if the dog hasn't trained for a while. Shepherd dogs that have taken a break in training and then go back to it usually show that they have pushed the learned exercises into the background and are hardly able to work out the instructions. However, shepherd dogs are often more willing to work and more diligent than their cattle dog counterparts, and for physical reasons they can stay in active service longer. Whereas many cattle dogs finish working when they are about eight years old, we see that, for instance, Malinois can work until they are 12 years old or sometimes even older.

TSB Evaluation of Phase C

The TSB (from the German *Triebveranlagung, Selbstsicherheit und Belastbarkeit* [Drive, Self-confidence, and Stress Tolerance]) evaluation describes the temperament characteristics of your dog for breeding purposes. The TSB has no influence over the final result of the IGP trial or a placing. To receive a TSB evaluation, your dog must have completed at least one protection phase.

The TSB evaluations employ the ratings Pronounced, Present, and Insufficient in assessment of drive, self-confidence, and stress tolerance:

- TSB Pronounced is given to a dog that displays a strong willingness to work, clear instinctive behavior, goal-oriented determination in the exercises, self-confident manner, unrestricted attention, and exceptional ability to handle stress.

- TSB Present is given to a dog that is restricted in his willingness to work, instinctive behavior, self-confidence, attention, and stress tolerance.

- TSB Insufficient is given to a dog that lacks willingness to work, instinctive behavior, self-confidence, and sufficient stress tolerance.

13

The Different Parts of Protection Work

As you train your dog in protection work leading up to the IGP trials, first consider the kind of terrain you will need to work on, then the requirements for each exercise. The terrain has six blinds, three set up on each side in a zigzag, staggered fashion. The distance between each of the three blinds in a row is 35 paces. In addition to the blinds, the host training center will have clearly marked areas where:

- The handler must stand to recall his dog out of the Bark and Hold blind;
- The decoy stands for the Escape and Defense, and where he has to stop;
- The dog is in a Down position for the Escape; and
- The handler must stand for the exercise called Attack on the Dog in Motion. (only for IGP 3)

At the trial, the first thing you do is report in—with an on-leash dog for IGP 1, and off leash for IGP 2 and 3. If you and your dog cannot report in in the proper manner—for instance, if your dog is not under control and runs—you may give up to three commands to recall your dog. If your dog does not come back after the third recall, then you and your dog are disqualified from Phase C due to lack of control. Note that in countries where the law prohibits the stick test, IGP tests can still be implemented. After reporting in successfully, take your dog to the start position for the first exercise: Search for the Decoy. In the IGP 1 trial, take your dog off leash; in IGP 2 and 3 trials, your dog should already be off leash. From that start position the judge will dispatch you and your dog.

The exercises in the IGP tests have different parts. While training, you should introduce these parts separately so your dog achieves maximum understanding as he builds up the protection work.

Phases in Protection Work

In IGP protection exercises there are several phases:

- Barking: during the Hold and Bark exercise, in which your dog has to bark continuously for about 20 seconds.
- Grip: where a quiet and full bite is desired; when your dog bites using his molars, he has a strong grip.
- Separation: in which your dog has to perform a fast "Out."
- Guarding: in which your dog has to watch the decoy attentively, silently, and powerfully.
- Pressure: in which your dog must quietly bite the decoy—without re-biting—even as the decoy exerts dynamic pressure on your dog and touches him with the soft stick.

Exercises in Protection Work

As in Phase B of IGP exercises, there are also different protection exercises:

Exercise 1: Search for the Decoy

Exercise 2: Hold and Bark

Exercise 3: Preventing an Escape by the Decoy

Exercise 4: Defense against an Attack in the Guarding Phase

Exercise 5: Back Transport (IGP 2 and 3)

Exercise 6: Attack On the Dog in the Back Transport (IGP 3)

Exercise 7: Attack On the Dog in Motion

Exercise 8: Side Transport to the Judge

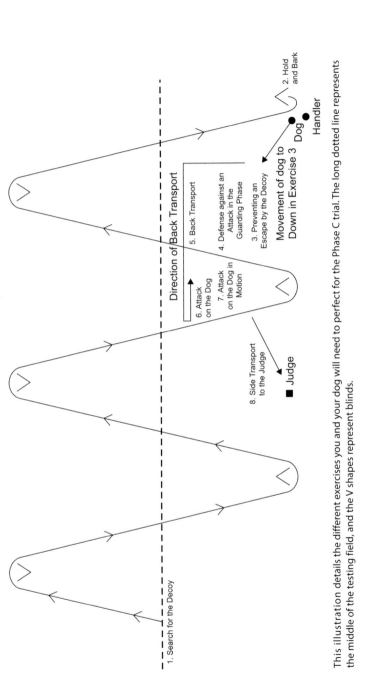

Direction of Back Transport

1. Search for the Decoy

2. Hold and Bark

Handler

Dog

Movement of dog to
Down in Exercise 3

3. Preventing an
Escape by the Decoy

4. Defense against an
Attack in the
Guarding Phase

5. Back Transport

6. Attack
on the Dog

7. Attack
on the Dog in
Motion

8. Side Transport
to the Judge

■ Judge

This illustration details the different exercises you and your dog will need to perfect for the Phase C trial. The long dotted line represents the middle of the testing field, and the V shapes represent blinds.

Exercise 1: Search for the Decoy

In all IGP levels, Search for the Decoy is the first protection exercise. In this exercise, your dog must systematically search the trial terrain for the decoy, who has hidden himself in a blind. The blind may simply be two doors placed at right angles to one another, or it may be a specially constructed blind tent. During the trial, you, the handler, walk directly down the middle of the field and use your voice and hand gestures to ask your dog to inspect the blinds. As you walk in a straight line, your dog moves from left to right across the field, searching for the decoy. Your dog will find the decoy standing up in the last blind.

In the IGP 1 trial, your dog only has to search one blind before he will find the decoy. You begin the exercise positioned with your on-leash dog at the starting position on the center line of the field even with the 6th blind (final blind). You unleash your dog when the exercise begins. In IGP 2, you and your off-leash dog begin the exercise between the second and third blinds, so that four side sweeps are possible. For IGP 3, you begin the exercise by positioning yourself with your off-leash dog in front of the first blind, so that six side sweeps are possible.

To begin performing the Search for the Decoy exercise in the IGP 2 and 3 trial, take the leash off your dog. In the execution of this exercise, you must move at a normal pace down an imaginary line that runs through the middle of the terrain. You are not permitted to stray from that middle line. The search begins with a brief command to "Search" augmented by the visual aid of you raising your left or right arm. Your dog must set out quickly and run to the indicated blind; goal-oriented, he must go around the blind tightly and attentively. When your dog executes the side sweep, call him back to you with "Here," and then use your arm gesture to direct him to the next blind and so on to the sixth blind, where the decoy is standing motionless in an unthreatening stance—invisible to the dog and to you—with his sleeve positioned at an angle. The sleeve acts as body protection

The Search for the Decoy exercise demands that dogs search the terrain systematically and carefully.

for the decoy. When your dog reaches the sixth blind, stop and give no further commands, verbal or visual.

Your dog will be evaluated on his ability to move quickly at your command in a goal-oriented, direct fashion. He should run tightly and attentively around the blinds. If he does not successfully find the decoy at the last blind on his first attempt, your dog is allowed two more attempts before he is terminated from the Phase C trial. As well, if you have to say, "Heel" at any time during the exercise, termination from Phase C results.

Exercise 2: Hold and Bark

When he reaches the sixth blind, your dog has to actively and attentively "hold" the decoy in place by barking continuously. This means he must guard the decoy and prevent his escape until you, the handler, arrives. Some dogs sit right in front of the decoy, but others stand, lie down, or jump—whatever your dog does, he may not jump on the decoy or grip him. If your dog bumps into or grips the decoy during the holding phase, the decoy must avoid making any

When your dog finds the decoy in the sixth blind, he must actively and attentively hold him in place by barking continuously.

defensive motions. During the Hold and Bark exercise, the decoy watches your dog but is not allowed to help motivate him. At this point in the trial, the decoy holds the soft stick at his side, facing downward.

When he has barked for about 20 seconds, at the instruction of the judge, approach your dog, stopping at a marked area that is about five paces away from where he is holding the decoy at bay. At the direction of the judge, ask your dog to come to you and assume the basic position. In IGP 1, you also have the option of stepping next to your dog, giving the command "Heel," and then taking him (off leash) to the area marked for calling the dog from the blind to you. Both possibilities are equally evaluated.

THE DIFFERENT PARTS OF PROTECTION WORK

When your dog is in the basic position, call the decoy out of the blind, and he will then walk at a normal pace over to the area marked for the Escape exercise. While this is happening, your dog must sit quietly (no more barking), straight and attentive in the basic position.

Exercise 3: Preventing an Escape by the Decoy

When the decoy has arrived at the marked area, make sure you are able to place your dog five paces away from the decoy's protection sleeve. As well, you must be able to clearly see the direction the decoy will take when he attempts to escape. On the judge's signal, take your free-heeling dog to the place where your dog must go down before the escape. Your dog must demonstrate a content, attentive, and concentrated Heeling exercise, positioning himself correctly and quickly at heel. Before you ask him to "Down," he must sit in the basic position, straight, calmly, and attentively. After you say, "Down," your dog should lie down quickly, directly, and confidently, all the while attentive to the decoy. At this point, leave your dog on watch in the Down position and go over to the sixth blind, but remain in visual contact with your dog, the decoy, and the judge.

At a sign from the judge, the decoy escapes using a quick and assertive pace, following a straight line, without running in an uncontrolled or exaggerated manner. During the escape, the sleeve must remain steady and your dog should be given the opportunity to execute his best possible grip. The decoy may not turn to face your dog at any time, but he can keep your dog in his field of vision. When the escape commences, command your dog to "Go on," and your dog should not hesitate but move directly to prevent the decoy's escape by means of a high dominance ratio and relatively fast hold, deploying an energetic and strong grip. Note that your dog may only grip the protection sleeve. If your dog remains in Down or does not prevent the escape through gripping or holding within 20 of the decoy's paces, he will be terminated from Phase C.

During the escape and prevention, the decoy must refrain from pulling the sleeve away from your dog. Once your dog has gripped, the decoy should continue to run along the same straight path, pulling the sleeve in close to his body. At the instruction of the judge, the decoy stops, at which point your dog must enter the Separation phase and release his grip almost immediately or after a brief transition period of about one to two seconds. You may give the command to "Out" almost immediately after the decoy stops. Remember to remain calm while saying "Out," without otherwise influencing your dog. After he releases his grip, your dog must remain close to the decoy and watch him attentively, kicking off the start of the next phase: Guarding.

If your dog leaves the decoy or you give a command so that your dog stays with the decoy, Phase C is terminated. Also, the decoy is not permitted to give assistance to your dog during the escape, such as offering the sleeve before the grip, verbal agitation, hitting the soft stick against his pants before or during the escape, taking up a limply held sleeve position, reducing the speed of the escape, or independently terminating the escape. If your dog does not release after the first permitted command, you will receive instructions from the judge to command "Out" again. If

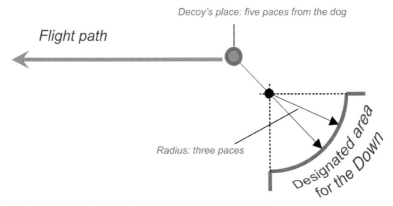

The place markings for Preventing an Escape by the Decoy.

he does not release his grip after a third "Out," your dog will be disqualified.

END OF THE DEFENSE EXERCISES

When defense exercises end, they must do so in such a manner that the judge has the opportunity to observe your dog's grip, "Out," and Guarding phase. This means the decoy should not turn his back to the judge and must maintain visual contact with him. The decoy should also minimize his resistance to your dog, reducing stimulation by not moving the sleeve. As well, the decoy should not carry the sleeve at a high angle as defense exercises terminate, but rather hold it in the same position it was in during the exercise. The decoy should hold the soft stick at his side, out of sight. The decoy is not allowed to help the dog during the Separation phase and after "Out," he should maintain eye contact with your dog. No other stimulation or help is permitted. To maintain eye contact with your dog, the decoy is allowed to turn if the dog circles him, but he should not make any sudden movements. If your dog doesn't release his grip, the decoy may not use the soft stick to encourage the dog to "Out." As well, if your dog leaves the decoy during the Guarding phase, the decoy may not encourage your dog to stay by making any sudden movements.

Exercise 4: Defense against an Attack in the Guarding Phase

After a Guarding phase of about five seconds, the decoy attacks your dog. You must not intervene as your dog defends himself by means of an energetic and strong grip. The dog may only grip the protection sleeve. As your dog grips the decoy's sleeve, the decoy pressures your dog by way of threatening stick gestures and driving him straight in one direction. The decoy may not turn at the start of this exercise. He must drive your dog in the same direction as he drives all the other dogs going through the trials, but he must never drive a dog toward his handler. The judge closely observes your dog when he is in the Pressure phase, especially making note of his activity and stability. The decoy wields the soft stick, making a threatening gesture with it above the sleeve without hitting your dog. Your dog must maintain a frontal and forward movement with corresponding resistance, without setting the sleeve in motion. All the while, the decoy carries his sleeve close in front of his body.

In this exercise, two tests are conducted to evaluate your dog's response to pressure put on him via the soft stick. Using the same level of intensity for all dogs, the decoy is to touch a spot either on the dog's shoulder or in the area of the withers. The decoy gives the first stick touch test after approximately four to five paces of the Pressure phase, the second test after an additional four to five paces. After the second test, the decoy exerts additional pressure on your dog without stick touches. Your dog has to be impartial during the Pressure phase and has to show a full, energetic, and above all constant grip during the entire defense exercise. At the instructions of the judge, the decoy stands still and your dog must enter another Separation phase and release his grip after a relatively brief transition period. You may give a command to "Out" within a reasonable amount of time, but you must remain calmly in place and not influence your dog in any other way. After he releases his grip on the decoy's sleeve, your dog is to remain close to the decoy and watch him attentively. Wait for the judge's signal before walking at a normal pace in the most direct way to your dog, and then ask him to assume the basic position by commanding "Heel." Do not take the soft stick from the decoy. Again, the decoy positions himself in such a manner that the judge is able to observe and evaluate your dog's behavior during the attack, Pressure phase, grip, release, and subsequent Guarding phase. Note that in the IGP 2 and 3 trial, the Defense against an Attack in the Guarding Phase exercise is repeated after the Attack On the Dog in Motion exercise.

During the Pressure phase, your dog must maintain an even bite on the sleeve (no re-biting!) even as the decoy applies dynamic pressure on him, increasing pressure from the soft stick.

Exercise 5: Back Transport

This exercise is only tested for in IGP 2 and 3. After Defense against an Attack in the Guarding Phase, the Back Transport of the decoy over a distance of about 30 normal paces follows. To begin this exercise, you may command your dog to "Heel" or "Transport." Also, order the decoy to move out, and accompany your off-leash dog, who is attentively watching the decoy as he follows the decoy five paces behind. This distance of five paces must be maintained throughout the Back Transport exercise. The judge determines the course of the transport. The decoy may not make any sudden moves during the exercise, and he must carry the soft stick and sleeve in such a way that he does not stimulate your dog: the soft stick especially has to be carried out of sight, and the decoy is to move at the same pace for every dog.

Exercise 6: Attack On the Dog in the Back Transport

This exercise is only tested in IGP level 3. During the Back Transport, the judge advises the decoy to attack your dog while everyone is in motion. The decoy performs the attack by making a dynamic left or right turn and running with purpose toward your dog. He should hold the soft stick above the sleeve and swing it in a threatening motion. Without encouragement from you and without hesitation, your dog is to defend himself with an energetic and strong grip. He may only grip the decoy's protection sleeve. As soon as your dog has a grip on the sleeve, you must stand still.

The decoy must intercept your dog with a flexibly positioned protection sleeve; he doesn't come to a halt when he reaches your dog. Upon interception, the decoy's body should, if possible, turn to catch your dog and match his movements with those of your dog. The decoy should avoid any additional movement of the sleeve. Once your dog grips, the decoy maneuvers your dog to the side and begins the Pressure phase, straight ahead in a predetermined direction.

After the decoy stops the Pressure phase, your dog has to release within a reasonable amount of time. You may also give the command "Out" within a reasonable amount of time. After the release, your dog is to remain close to the decoy and watch him attentively. At the judge's instruction, you may walk at a normal pace directly to your dog and ask him to assume the basic position with the command "Heel." Then, take the soft stick from the decoy.

You and your dog now conduct the Side Transport of the Decoy to the Judge, over a distance of about 20 paces. You are permitted to ask your dog to "Heel." Your dog is to move along at the right side of the decoy, so that he is between you and the decoy. During the transport, your dog has to be attentive to the decoy, but he may not crowd him, jump on him, or grip. When you arrive in front of the judge, stop. At this point, give the soft stick to the judge and report out, thereby ending the first part of Phase C.

Exercise 7: Attack On the Dog in Motion

At the beginning of this exercise for IGP 3, the judge will tell you to go with your dog to the spot marked on the middle line at the level of the first blind line. Your dog should heel and be attentive to you; he should be concentrating and demonstrating a contented demeanor as he moves along beside you, straight, shoulder in line with your knee. When you reach the level of the first blind, stop and turn around. At this point, ask your dog to "Sit," and your dog should assume the basic position, calmly, straightly, and attentively facing forward. You may hold your dog by the collar, but you may not stimulate your dog in any way. At a sign from the judge, the decoy leaves the assigned blind and moves at a running pace to the center line without breaking stride. With threatening words and gestures, the decoy attacks the dog and you, the handler, from the front with the soft stick. The decoy should ignore your shouts as he runs toward you. As soon as the decoy is about 50 to 40 paces (for IGP 3) in front of you and your dog, and at a sign from the judge, release your dog.* Without hesitation and after one command to "Go on," your dog is to effectively prevent the attack through a high dominance factor and relatively quick speed. He may only grip the decoy's protection sleeve. You, the handler, may not leave your place.

The decoy should intercept your dog, continue on and present the sleeve to him, not holding the sleeve close to his body. Upon intercepting your dog, the decoy's body should, if possible, turn to catch your dog and move according to the dog's movements to maintain the momentum. The decoy may not run around your dog. Once your dog grips, the decoy maneuvers him out of motion to the side and begins to conduct the Pressure phase. It is imperative that the decoy avoids overrunning the dog.

During the Pressure phase, you and the decoy may not influence your dog, and during the entire defense exercise, your dog must display a full, energetic, and above all constant grip. At the direction of the judge, the decoy stops and the dog enters the Separation phase and should release his grip after a brief transition

* In IGP 1 and 2, the decoy will remain mid-field after the last defense exercise and the handler will pick up the dog and heel away down the mid-line of the field to a distance of approximately 33 yards (30 m) away for the IGP 1, and 44 yards (40 m) away for the IGP 2. Then the handler stops and turns towards the helper, whereupon the judge will signal the exercise to begin.

When under pressure from the decoy, your dog must be impartial to him. Your dog must demonstrate a full, energetic, and above all constant grip throughout the defense exercises.

period. You may give a command to "Out" after a reasonable amount of time, but you must stay calm and not influence your dog in any other way. After the release, your dog is to remain close to the decoy and watch him attentively. At the judge's instruction, walk at a normal pace directly toward your dog and command, "Heel," so that he takes the basic position. Take the soft stick from the decoy.

You and your dog now conduct a side transport of the decoy over a distance of about 20 paces to the judge. You are permitted to command "Heel," and your dog is to move along at the right side of the decoy, between you and the decoy. During the transport, your dog is to be attentive to the decoy, but he may not crowd him, jump on him, or grip. Your little group halts in front of the judge, where you hand the soft stick to the judge and report out, thereby ending Phase C.

At the instruction of the judge, you now walk with your off-leash dog about five paces from the decoy and there ask your dog to assume the basic position. Put your dog on leash and walk him to the place where the critique will be given. In the meantime, the decoy receives instructions from the judge to leave the field.

14

Advanced Decoy Techniques

The decoy is the most important person in protection work. A skilled decoy can train dogs that have courage as well as dogs that aren't very courageous; a bad decoy can frighten or discourage even the most courageous dog. So a good decoy is worth his weight in gold at your training club! The good decoy is aware of his enormous responsibility to the handlers and their dogs. He knows he has to be in good physical and mental condition—protection work is heavy and tiring.

That said, the best decoy is not always the strongest and heaviest person in the club. Heavy people often use too much power in decoy work. Remember that the decoy's job demands strength and flexibility, as well as fine insight into dog behavior. Whether or not you can lift a dog off the ground for a long time, or whether or not you can swing a dog around, is unimportant. What is important is knowing how to catch a dog the right way and at the right moment during an attack. The decoy must be able to judge the movements of a dog, and he must be able to react speedily.

The decoy's personality also plays a big part in how successful he is in his role. Consider the mental pressure a decoy brings to bear on a dog. Whether a dog fails or is built up correctly depends on him. He has to judge if he is handling a hard dog too roughly,

A good decoy develops his routine through an extensive physical and mental practice with different dogs and breeds.

or maybe a soft dog too carefully. He has to be a quiet person and needs full control of his muscles in order to react well. Besides that, the good decoy knows and accepts that he must always lose to the dog and handler. To make the dog strong, the decoy always has to be inferior to the dog. Further, he may not differentiate between the dog of a friend and that of a stranger or an enemy. He must handle every dog in the same way, and he may not give an advantage to any dog.

In addition to having the characteristics described above, the decoy must also be knowledgeable. He must have the dog smarts and the experience necessary to prepare a dog for protection exercises, not to mention the people/training knowledge to conduct his affairs with handlers and instructors properly. For example, when coordinating training with instructors and handlers, he has to remember his "place" as the decoy. He cannot simply have a talk on the training field with the handler. During bite work, the decoy is a rascal, and he has to behave that way during training. Handlers have to treat decoys on the training field as bad guys so that the dogs are not confused. For your dog, bite work is serious: he knows he has to keep an eye on the bad guy. The instructor is always present during bite work to give instructions to the decoy and the handler. The good decoy knows never to give instructions during bite work, and he has to obey instructions given to him without complaining.

In this chapter, we describe the equipment decoys use when working with dogs, as well as the techniques they employ to help dogs progress through protection training.

Full Control

It is important for the decoy to be able to control himself and assess where and when a dog is biting into the sleeve. He also has to be able to see if a dog is biting poorly, and then he should immediately react and give the dog the opportunity to improve his grip. A good decoy also knows how to catch a storming dog, which is so important to the well-being of both dog and decoy. A wrong catch, for instance with the sleeve against the decoy's chest, may block the dog and seriously injure his neck. An adept decoy uses his sleeved arm much like a spring that catches the first hint of the bite, and then he employs his entire body to redirect the power of the dog's advance, turning according to the direction and speed of the dog, and taking care not to force himself on the dog as he does so. A good decoy knows not to keep the sleeve too close to his chest and to pay attention to his knees as he catches the dog. As well, the well-versed decoy knows how to keep himself under control during the moment the dog has bitten into the sleeve: he must not push the dog back too strongly, as this can damage the dog's neck muscles or neck vertebrae. Although the dog may be pushed back a short distance, a good decoy knows never to walk over him. This need for total control begins when a decoy starts

Decoy work demands mental and physical flexibility, as well as knowledge about dog behavior.

his training. A person starting out as a decoy should have both a degree of talent for the work as well as correct training from expert instructors and other helpers.

The Equipment

CLOTHES FOR PROTECTION WORK

Decoys must wear the right protection clothes to be safe on the training field. Your training club should not economize on these, but we see that happen often. An IGP dog training club's board may come to the conclusion that it is "good enough" to use a cheaper pair of protection pants, but these people are not the ones who have to get out on the field and train with the dogs. Most decoys are volunteers, and clubs or dog training organizations must step up and give them everything they need to be safe and comfortable in their work. Most dogs bite on the protection sleeve, but that rogue bite on the leg should not result in an injury. Decoys must always don the proper protection clothes, even when they think they can work risk-free with only a sleeve. As well, remember that dogs will begin to recognize the "look" of a decoy; deviation from this look can confuse dogs. An overly aggressive dog that does not recognize the decoy without his protection clothes might cause some damage.

Other parts of a decoy's outfit include his sleeve and tug, or bite pillow. None of these items should have loose ends or be in any way frayed on the outside—damage like that can be dangerous for a biting dog. A dog's canine teeth can get hung up in loose ends and break. Training clubs should always be monitoring the equipment, making sure it is safe for decoys and dogs.

According to the IGP testing regulations, the decoy must be equipped with a protection suit, protection sleeve, and a soft stick. The protection sleeve must have a grip bar, the cover made of natural jute (burlap) fiber. In the IGP program, dogs only have to do bite work with the sleeve. In other programs, such as the French and Belgian Ringsport programs and the program of the Royal Dutch Police Dog Association (KNPV), bite work is also conducted on the decoy's leg, and therefore these programs require different protection gear.

The IGP testing regulations require that decoys wear full protection suits, both bite pants and jacket. In IGP training, most decoys use bite pants that are rather like overalls made of suede or leather. We prefer the quilted leather bite pants because they do not soak up water when it is raining, and they also can be used in shrubs or tall grass during practice outside the training field. Another advantage to these pants is that they are easy to clean, and with regular greasing are usable for many years. Suede bite pants, however, are lighter and thinner than their leather counterparts, giving the decoy better maneuverability. The downside of the suede pants is that they offer less protection, and they easily pick up water and mud and therefore are prone to getting heavy and dirty. Note that regardless of the material, all bite pants and jackets should be free of buckles, which are a source of danger for decoys and dogs.

The protection clothes and equipment used by a decoy in advanced protection exercises: a full protection suit, bite pants and jacket, a protection sleeve, and a soft stick.

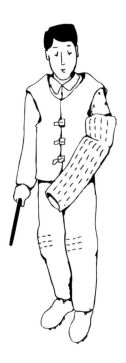

Another key part of the protection get-up is shoes. Decoys must keep their feet firmly on the ground during protection work, so it's important that the possibility of slipping is minimized by footwear. Decoys should therefore never go to work wearing smooth-soled gym shoes. Instead, protection shoes should have a rugged tread, or even cleats. Note, however, that terrain should be considered relative to footwear: if training on a very hard surface, cleats are not effective. As well, trainee decoys should not use footwear with cleats because they are not yet in full control of their movements, and there is a risk of stepping on dogs' toes, which can be mentally disastrous for beginning and young dogs. Trainee decoys should use climbing boots that have a good, heavy tread.

BITE TUGS, RAGS, AND PILLOWS
When teaching the beginner dog to bite correctly, we use many different pieces of excellent equipment: short or long tugs, with

one or two handles; bite-training pillows with three handles; prey-drive training rags; puppy bite builders; advanced puppy bite developers; young-dog sleeves; and so on. Of course, all of these tugs and rags are made of all kinds of materials—jute, French linen, leather, and even fire hoses. With all of these options, you can leave behind the old-fashioned, rolled-up burlap sack!

BITE SLEEVES

The sleeves for IGP training are constructed of a plastic or leather tube with a cup positioned as a protection cover for the decoy's upper arm. The so-called "bite-bar" sleeve has a blade or bar on the outside of the tube that provides a V-shaped biting surface. There is a handle inside the tube that allows the decoy to hold the sleeve in place. An expendable jute sleeve cuff fits over the hard tube; this cover can be stuffed to make it thicker or softer. You can also choose thicker covers made of rope. Again, your club should monitor protection wear and ensure that worn-out covers are replaced to ensure dogs' teeth or gums are not damaged during protection work. And, like the protection suit, sleeves should be free of buckles.

There are left-handed as well as right-handed sleeves. Before buying one, the decoy should try out several different ones to find the one that suits the thickness and length of his arm. As well, there are puppy sleeves, which do not have the interior leather/plastic tube, but do have a handle. Such soft and pliable sleeves are specially designed for training young and novice dogs.

SOFT STICK

The soft stick used in protection work is about 23 inches (60 cm) long. It has a flexible plastic core and is padded with felt and covered with leather aero material, which provides an optimal balance between firmness and flexibility. In countries where laws prohibit the stick test, the IGP trials can be implemented without it.

Technique

USING THE SLEEVE

A beginner decoy often only moves his lower arm during an action, after the dog has bitten. With downward movements, such a decoy will keep the dog working on and turning around over the field. This is a nasty experience for the persistent dog, because the jute sleeve cover moves around between his front and canine teeth until the decoy quits. Using this method, there is no "smooth line" in the dog's fight with the decoy.

An experienced and talented decoy, on the other hand, will catch the dog between the middle of the sleeve and the elbow and, during the fight, keeps his lower arm as much as possible at a right angle to his upper arm. As the dog bites in, the decoy keeps the sleeve neither too high nor too low, and always away from his torso.

From the beginning of his training, the decoy has to learn to control where he allows the dog to bite the sleeve by paying attention at the moment the dog bites in. By moving a bit at the last moment, a good decoy can shift the sleeve so the dog is biting in about four to six inches (10–15 cm) below the elbow on his lower arm. This kind of maneuvering becomes routine through frequent training. That particular location on the sleeve is the sweet spot, because if a dog bites in there, the decoy has the right leverage in his arm to pivot and handle even heavy dogs like a Giant Schnauzer, Rottweiler, or German shepherd male. By ensuring that the dog bites the sleeve in that spot, the decoy ensures his ability to keep his arm locked in a square formation during the action. If the decoy allows the dog to bite at the end of the sleeve, the dog will have greater leverage, and it will be impossible for the decoy to keep his arm still and squared.

After the fight, the decoy should stand still, and he should block the sleeve, or hold the sleeved upper arm against his torso. The better the decoy assumes this position—keeping that sleeve

The decoy has to catch the dog in between the middle of the sleeve and his elbow. During the fight, he should always keep his lower arm at a right angle to his upper arm.

If the dog bites at the end of the sleeve, he can maneuver the decoy's arm like a lever.

as still as possible—the better the release—or "Out"—the dog will perform, and there will be less of a chance that the dog will re-bite.

Both in attacks from a short distance and from a longer distance, the decoy must always approach and catch the dog straight on, in front. The sleeve should never be moved higher, lower, or to the side once the dog has jumped off the ground, as this could ruin the timing for the bite and upset the dog's training.

BODY TECHNIQUE

When people outside the IGP training world are watching a decoy as he threatens and turns, smoothly transitioning from one position to another, they may believe that a decoy's work is pretty easy. Nothing is less true! The decoy has perfected his routine through

During the fight, the decoy should keep the sleeve in front
of his torso and as still as possible.

extensive physical and mental exercise with different dogs and
breeds.

Decoy work is very tiring. Even the use of the threatening
voice takes a lot of energy. In the beginning, every decoy can feel
which groups of muscles in his body are being affected by this
heavy work. It is important to train these groups of muscles by
performing special exercises, especially working the muscles of the
underarms, neck, legs, and back.

As we said earlier, during the fight, the decoy needs to keep the
sleeve as still as possible in front of his torso, so he has to move
other parts of his body in order to be an active opponent for the
dog. After all, a dog doesn't need to use his teeth on a still and
motionless decoy! Because the decoy's torso and arms must remain
as still as possible, the decoy's "fighting" moves—pivots, driving
backward, and dog-catching—all stem from the decoy's hips and
legs.

During a fight, the decoy's upper body—sleeve kept in front—
has to be passive and turn, actually hinge, on both of the decoy's
hips. His legs support and move the torso as the decoy turns in
different directions. This technique, if discussed well in theory
and demonstrated several times in practice, can only be mastered
by the decoy after many weeks of repetition. Only by practicing frequently—first without and later on with the dog—can the
decoy come to control this necessary body technique.

LEG TECHNIQUE

Much depends on the decoy's leg technique, especially when he is
driving the dog backward (or forward, from the decoy's perspective). After he catches the dog, the decoy and dog make a quarter
or half turn (depending on the speed at which the dog is coming in), and then the decoy drives the dog some paces diagonally
backward. After this, another turn follows with a shorter amount
of driving backward, and then the handler commands his dog to
"Out." At a trial, the decoy has to ensure that he is stopping in
profile or in front of the judge so the judge can assess the dog's
grip, release, and Guarding phase.

The decoy drives the dog backward at an angle, either to
the left or the right. Should the decoy push the dog straight
backward, he would inevitably step on the dog's toes. At the
same time, the dog's traction power could pull the decoy over
his center of gravity, making him fall over, or worse, fall on the
dog. The decoy can prevent this kind of fumbling by keeping the
dog between his legs, which he moves diagonally one ahead of
the other, front leg first. As he moves in this fashion, the decoy
also bends his knees, keeping his center of gravity closer to the
ground. In this position, the decoy feels stable in his movements
and minimizes his chances of falling. This driving backward
must not be done over too great a distance and has to be performed using supple, not shaking, movements in order to spare
the dog's neck.

The decoy's body and leg techniques are important to the dog's safety during a fight.

THE PIVOT

The decoy's hallmark move is the manner in which he catches a dog during an attack from a distance. The decoy knows that he must avoid a head-on collision with the dog. His trick is to smoothly catch the dog as soon as he bites by slipping his body mass—his center of gravity—out from behind the sleeve to the left or right. With this movement, the decoy allows the dog's inertia to propel a safe catch.

When the decoy attacks the dog, he approaches him at a speed of about 4.5 miles (6 km) per hour; at the same time, the dog is advancing on the decoy at a speed of between 12 and 19 miles (20 and 30 km) per hour (depending on the breed). When the dog and decoy make contact, the power of the impact on the dog's jaws and (cervical) vertebrae and muscles is enormous: the kinetic energy is about 1,350 Newton meters, or 300 pound-feet! When working with fast dogs, therefore, it is much better if the decoy stops and stands still just before the dog grips his sleeve. This way of catching fast dogs, like Malinois, prevents many dog injuries.

The decoy's catching technique is a combination of arm, body, and leg movements, and it demands a lot of concentration. It is rather like a pirouette performed by a dancer. It takes only a few seconds in real time, but here we will attempt to break it down into all of its parts.

First, the decoy runs toward the dog, keeping the sleeve squared but somewhat in front of his torso. At the moment that both jaws of the dog are placed around the sleeve (the teeth are already in the jute), the decoy turns on his front leg—to the left or the right—and the space is partially taken up by the dog's body. After the pivot, the decoy's back leg carries the weight of the airborne dog and, with the sleeve, ensures that the decoy doesn't walk over the dog. The sleeved arm of the decoy acts like a spring for the dog's body. As the decoy practices, he will decide which side to turn to in order to ensure the smoothest pivot—which way the turn goes and how it is executed also depends on how the dog approaches and the decoy's skill and athletic ability.

If the decoy has not mastered this technique, or if he reacts too late, the dog will hit the sleeved arm—as well as the decoy's body and knees—at full speed. This kind of collision can be very dangerous for the dog and painful for the decoy. A dog that trains with a decoy who controls the pivot very well will learn he can come in harder and faster every training session. If this dog then trains with a decoy who has not mastered the pivot and thus experiences a head-on collision, the dog will experience a very painful jolt during this exercise!

WORKING WITH THE SOFT STICK

The soft stick must be used during IGP examinations, so it is important to use it in training, too. In countries where laws prohibit the stick test, the IGP trials can be deployed without it.

The decoy keeps the stick firmly in hand, his thumb in the upright position, which helps him direct the stick. He always has to know where the stick is touching the dog and to keep the stick under control. The decoy must not strike out rashly with the stick; he must always be poised, controlled, and directed. He has to remember that the dog's joints and spinal column are very sensitive to pressure from the soft stick.

The decoy only touches the dog with the soft stick after the dog has a firm grip, and he doesn't always stop the fight immediately after using the stick on the dog. (Variation in training with the soft stick prevents the dog from predicting that the fight will always be over after the soft stick is employed and releasing his grip regardless of the handler's command to "Out.") The decoy should be careful when touching the dog with the stick and remember that it is only used to test the dog's toughness, not to see how high the dog's pain threshold is, or to find out how much a dog can take before he will release. Also, the decoy should be careful when he threatens with the stick: a flexible stick can injure a dog—he must not, for example, whip the dog in the face or in another sensitive area. When employing the soft stick, the decoy steadies his movements by using his entire stick-wielding arm, thereby preventing injuries to the dog.

The decoy is not allowed to suddenly reach out and touch the dog's side with the soft stick. After biting in, the dog must clearly be able to see the soft stick coming toward him from above. So, after some "threatening hits," the decoy uses the soft stick to touch the dog two times, but not in succession and not too firmly.

The IGP testing regulations state that the decoy has to pressure the dog by way of threatening stick gestures and driving him backward. While this is happening, the judge observes the dog closely. When the decoy conducts the two stick-pressure tests, he may only do so by using the soft stick to touch the dog on his shoulders or the area of his withers. So, for the decoy, it is absolutely necessary to know dog anatomy.

A well-trained working dog has developed muscles. His back and rib cage are protected by the long dorsal muscle (*musculus longissimus dorsi*) and the wide dorsal muscle (*musculus latissimus dorsi*). The rib cage itself offers protection to the dog's internal organs. The kidneys, however, are unprotected. The correct place for the soft stick to land is diagonally over the back, just behind the dog's shoulder blades. Because the decoy is administering soft-stick pressure from the side, the soft stick contacts the dog at a 30° angle to his body.

After the dog bites into the protection sleeve, the decoy makes sure that the dog can see the soft stick coming down on him from above. The dog should not be surprised with pressure from the soft stick.

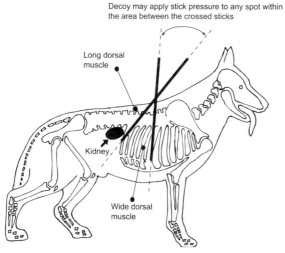

The parts of the dog's body where the decoy may apply soft-stick pressure.

This is a clear example of a wrongly placed and very dangerous hit to the dog's unprotected kidneys (with an old-fashioned bamboo stick).

The dog must become used to soft-stick pressure in order to go through the IGP trials, and so during training you must build his confidence in the face of the instrument slowly and carefully. You should never, for example, flip your dog over and hit him with the soft stick. Generally, it is difficult to know what the right dose of well-placed touches is. This is where a good instructor and a skilled decoy come in handy. The good decoy only attains such knowledge through much practice and experience.

Trial Decoys

In IGP's *International Utility Dogs Regulations*, we find the prerequisites for employment as a decoy in Phase C trials. The Phase C decoy is the assistant to the judge on the day of the trial, and before the trial work for Phase C begins, the decoy receives instructions from the judge. For his personal protection, as well as due to insurance liability, whether in training or on a given trial day or competitions, the decoy must wear protective clothing: protection pants, protection jacket, sleeve and cup, gloves (if necessary), and weather-proof shoes that are suitable for the ground conditions and that secure stance and ensure good traction.

The decoy must perform the work in accordance with the judge's instructions and must also follow the instructions of handlers during the Search for the Decoy exercise and the disarming in accordance with the trial rules. Furthermore, he must give handlers the opportunity to position their dogs in the correct heel position for the Side and/or Back Transport exercises.

In the IGP regulations governing the conduct of trial decoys, you will find that during a trial, the judge evaluates the level of training and the quality of the dog being presented—based on the dog's drives, stress level, self-confidence, and obedience—and the decoy must treat all dogs and handlers equally. This equal treatment helps the judge ensure that dogs are able to address each of the individual elements of the most important evaluation criteria for Phase C: stress level, self-confidence, drives, obedience, and grip quality. The decoy must give every dog the opportunity to secure a "good grip," for example, and the decoy places the proper pressure on each dog when the dog's stress level is tested. As it is written in the regulations: "The helper [decoy] must strive to have the most uniform level of helper work, so that the requirements of the evaluation are met."

Group Training

It was once customary to introduce dogs to a decoy during a group training exercise called Circle Agitation. However, today, only dogs with lower drives train with this method. Most often, all dogs training for protection work are built up individually. That said, group training still requires a description in this manual.

In group training, handlers stand with their dogs in a big circle in the middle of the training field, between the blinds. The distance between the dogs is such that they do not hinder one another. If you are using a choke chain on your dog, it should not be set to "choke"—indeed, wide leather dollars or a padded agitation harness with a Y-shaped chest plate is much better—and you hold your dog on a short leash. The handlers have to stay in their places and ensure that the decoy has enough room to do his work. The decoy works on the outside of the circle, never inside. If he were to operate inside the circle, it is possible that dogs could attack him from the side or the back.

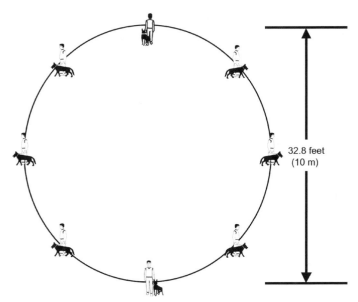

32.8 feet
(10 m)

Individual handlers and their dogs take up positions around a big circle for the agitation and bite work exercise.

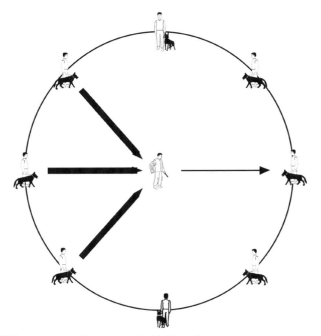

ERROR! The decoy should never work inside the circle during group exercises because of the danger of a dog attack from the side or back.

Before the dogs enter the training area, the decoy (completely outfitted and equipped with a leather rag or a bite tug with two handles) should already be positioned in one of the blinds. Once all are assembled, the decoy emerges from the blind, bent over and acting very afraid as he walks around the circle. First he walks carefully toward a dog and then walks away quickly and fearfully. After approaching every dog in this manner, he disappears into a different blind from the one he came from. This exercise is repeated a few times, after which the decoy disappears into a blind and the dogs leave the field.

If a dog is showing fear or reserve, the decoy will pass him without agitation. Such dogs need a bit more time; a good decoy knows not to hurry these dogs and not to pay attention to them because that will only exacerbate their fear.

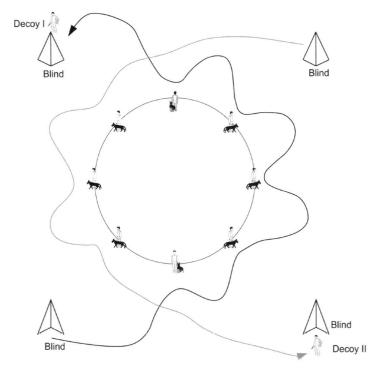

This is one possible training scheme for a group exercise with two decoys who come out of the blinds in turns.

One of the keys to this exercise is the decoy's use of different blinds, which teaches dogs to pay attention to all the blinds, which in turn makes it easier to teach them the Search for the Decoy exercise. Some training groups also choose to use multiple decoys during this exercise. The decoys take turns: one works the circle while the others hide in various blinds, waiting for their turn to approach the dogs.

Individual Training

In today's protection training sessions, dogs and handlers go to the training field to do their exercises individually. The advantage to training in this way is that they are not distracted by dogs barking behind and beside them. Also, the instructions, commands, or corrections of the instructor are easier to hear, and the exercises can be tailored to fit the dog. Individual sessions are necessarily shorter than group sessions; no one has to wait to take a turn or for another dog and handler to be ready. Short and frequent training sessions, as opposed to long, drawn-out ones, tend to increase the dog's level of learning.

The first exercise you practice with your dog and a decoy when training individually involves a leather rag on a leash. Keep your dog on leash and do not say anything; his attention should be focused on the decoy, who is enticing your dog by moving the leash and rag quickly to the left or right. After a while, the decoy allows your dog to catch the rag. At this point, you can quietly praise your dog and run some circles with him and his "prey," the rag. When your dog loses interest in the rag and drops it, you must prevent him from picking the rag up again. At this point in the training exercise, the decoy approaches your dog in a bent and frightened pose, takes the rag, and runs away. Repeat this exercise two or three times. In the end, instead of having to give the rag up to the decoy, your dog is allowed to take his "prey" with him to the car or his crate, where you exchange the rag for a treat.

During bite work with a rag, the rag will get wet. This is a good thing because when the rag is slippery, your dog has to bite down hard to get a purchase on the leather. If he does not employ a strong bite, your dog will begin to notice that he loses the fight over and over again because the decoy is able to pull the rag out of his mouth. Slowly, your dog's bite will become stronger and stronger.

The Correct Bite

During the first biting exercises, the decoy determines how your dog is biting and what kind of help he needs to learn to bite correctly. If your dog's bite is not a technically correct grip—so, not a full bite with the rag fully in his mouth, but one that only employs his front teeth or canines—the decoy continues to train him with the leather rag. The decoy helps your dog learn to grip correctly by pushing the wet rag to the back of your dog's mouth during the exercises. As soon as the bite is correct, your dog is allowed to take the rag/prey and show off. In this way, your dog begins to learn that he is only allowed to take the rag away when he grips correctly.

When your dog's bite is correct, the decoy exchanges the rag for a prey-drive training tug. He approaches your dog at a 45° angle until he is just in front of him, then he turns 90° and walks away. The decoy then performs the same exercise, but this time, as he passes in front of your dog and walks away, you allow your dog to bite the tug. You must softly encourage your dog to do so. The decoy then catches your dog and moves the tug correctly so he has a good experience biting in; a good decoy will know the right moment to let go of the tug, allowing your dog to take it and proudly walk away, his ears ringing with your praise.

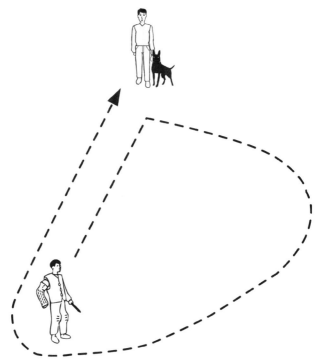

In this bite-training sequence, the decoy encounters the dog and his handler at a 45° angle and walks away at a right angle. The dog is allowed to bite after the decoy has passed him once or twice. The arrow indicates where the dog bites the decoy.

Waiting Dogs

Most of the time, dogs left alone tied up to stakes or trees near the training field are an endless source of chaotic barking and whining. When handlers leave their dogs this way, or in cars alone, they are in danger of warping their dogs' good character. The dogs determine their own behavior when they are left alone like this, and often they are so worn out from barking that they are too tired to train when it is their turn, and they cannot focus on the training.

A Schutzhund is a quiet, self-confident dog that at the right moment can switch into action, and still be able to survey the whole situation around him. When dogs are left on their own, they can become distrustful, sharp, rowdy characters with foam on their jaws. From the start, it is important to teach your dog to remain quiet after each exciting training exercise. A powerful command from you will gather your dog under your control after exercises and as you leave the field. Your dog should learn that there is no reason to bark before starting protection work or after the exercises are complete; you must demand obedience.

When you bring a young or novice dog to the training field, first take him to the area around the field where the protection work is taking place. Stay with your dog and keep him busy. Allow him to watch the handlers and dogs at work, and reward him with treats if he is interested but quiet. When you teach your dog to wait quietly on the outskirts of the training field, you are also showing him that everything related to protection work has to be done in a quiet way.

Decoy Attitude and Stimulation

Agitating a dog that is new to protection training should always be done with care. At first, the decoy must not go after the dog with a lot of yelling, threatening behavior, and show of power. Instead, he has to arouse the dog's suspicions by his attitude. To accomplish this, decoys study how wild animals related to dogs demonstrate how they are feeling or indicate their social rank. When we look at wolves, for example, we see that the dominant male impresses his pack mates with his higher rank through body language: the facial expression, the hard look at an opponent; the tail carried high; the hair standing on end (making him look bigger); and movement, walking around with high, stiff, stretched legs, are the most common expressions of superior strength and status in wolves. The opposite behavior—crouching to look smaller, approaching from a low position, and turning away the head—expresses submission, and a wolf that behaves this way shows that he feels lesser than the others. At first, the decoy must show submission.

In the Preventing an Escape by the Decoy exercise, as soon as the decoy flees, the handler lets the dog bite.

When he begins agitating your dog, the decoy plays at being submissive, taking a nonthreatening stance. He has to approach your dog hesitantly the first few times, almost cringing and with his face turned away. Now and again, he takes a few steps backward to stimulate your dog's attention. He does not approach your dog too closely, and when he is a few yards away, he definitively walks away to hide in another blind. On the way to that new blind, he may change his posture so he is more upright, and he might also make some noise. But when your dog can see him, he has to look as though he is fleeing. When the decoy walks away, he stimulates your dog's passion for the chase. In fact, if you were not holding your dog tightly, he would run after the decoy at this point.

A decoy who starts a dog out by walking right up to him and threatening him forces that dog into deciding whether to flee or attack. This should never happen in the first stages of training. We first have to teach the dog that he is always the winner on the training field and that the decoy is a fearful, easy-to-defeat rascal, who quickly runs away.

Handler Attitude and Stimulation

How you, the handler, hold your dog during exercises with a decoy is very important. Normally your dog can be kept on a leash that is about 10 feet (3 m) long. You should not hold the leash taut, but keep your dog on the same length of leash throughout training exercises. This way, the decoy can easily determine how far to pull or push if he wants the leash to be taut. Remember that during the bite work you should receive all instructions from the instructor, not the decoy.

Obedience is the first step to proper protection work. If you have a hectic dog, he may, when acting on impulse, bite the first thing that appears before his snout, perhaps even your leg! If your dog is like this, you must keep him on your left side, against your left knee with a hand on his collar or harness. Put your left leg one step ahead of your dog so you don't lose your balance—whatever happens, keep your dog's neck close to your knee.

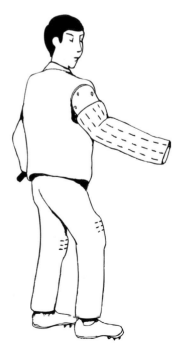

When training for the first attack from a distance, the decoy yells and walks away from the dog, positioning the sleeve at the side of his body.

Your attitude during agitation (and further bite work) is also very important. Throughout the bite exercises, you must stand still with your dog on leash—the decoy does most of the real work—but this does not mean that you have to be silent. Encourage your dog when he reacts to the decoy, tell your dog he is a "Good boy" when he barks at the decoy, and make sure your dog notices the praise. When your dog barks, he needs you to encourage him loudly and, when possible, to pet him to show clearly that you are satisfied. But don't distract his attention from the decoy with your praise!

When it's time to send the decoy away, do so using your voice. A clearly spoken "Beat it, man!" shows your dog that you are actively involved in sending the rascal away. After all, for your dog, this is a serious game, and you must show that you take it seriously.

15

Raising Dogs for Protection Work

Provided that you have the necessary self-control, it is possible for you to teach your young dog skills that he can use later when he begins training for protection work. Make sure you spend those puppy training moments carefully so that you educate your dog correctly. Take your dog everywhere with you and make him used to people and other dogs and animals. The biggest mistake you can make during your dog's puppyhood is to isolate him from other people, fearful that he will become everybody's friend. If you allow your dog to get to know other people and animals, he will grow up to be a sociable, well-behaved dog, the kind of dog that is perfect for IGP training. The Schutzhund does not attack others, and he is not a foolish dog that cannot behave among other people and animals.

Dogs that are suspicious of strangers in their youth—or that show their teeth, bark, or raise their hackles when a stranger is tempting or teasing them—do so out of fear; they carry a germ of cowardice in them. A dog that has been socialized will be friendly with strangers and will go to them when tempted—this is the better behavior of the two.

There are four important exercises you should consider when raising a puppy intended for IGP training:

- Exercise 1: Bark on Command
- Exercise 2: Be Silent
- Exercise 3: Puppy Bite Work
- Exercise 4: Out

These exercises can form part of the education of a young dog that is five months and older.

Exercise 1: Bark on Command

It is helpful if a novice dog training to be a Schutzhund already knows how to bark on command. The first thing to do is find something that stimulates your young dog to bark. Be creative! For example, hold your puppy's full food bowl high enough that he can smell the food but cannot reach it. When the pup becomes impatient for the food, he may start to bark. Alternatively, holding a favorite toy or ball up high can make a puppy bark if you wait long enough. The frustration at not being given that toy will eventually make him bark.

Once you've figured out how to make your puppy bark, reward every bark with some food from the bowl or a brief bit of play with the toy. Do not forget to praise your puppy, "Good boy!" but do not add a command to bark just yet. Adding the command to the action and praise will come later when your dog begins barking at the food bowl or toy with no encouragement from you. After the reward and praise are given, put the food bowl or toy away, wait a bit, and then begin the exercise anew. Again, after your puppy squeaks or barks, reward him. In the beginning, reward your puppy after he barks two or three times; later on, let him bark for longer before giving the reward. If your puppy does not bark easily, do not repeat the exercise over and over, or he will not like doing it anymore.

If your dog does not bark easily, keep practicing the same exercise with the food bowl or the toy, whichever one elicited the first

If you tantalize your dog with his favorite toy for long enough, he will begin to bark.

When your dog squeaks or barks, reward him. At first, give him his reward if he barks two or three times. Later in training, have him bark for a longer period before rewarding him.

bark or squeak. As soon as he is barking at the sight of the raised bowl or toy, add the command for barking, "Bark," accompanied by a discreet hand or head signal. For instance, when your dog is watching you and you are giving the command to bark, tap your forefinger and thumb of the same hand together. The dog will soon associate that signal with the command and later react to the signal alone with loud barking.

Exercise 2: Be Silent

A Schutzhund must be able to bark, but he must also know how to be silent when necessary. Because silence does not demand physical effort, you can teach a puppy to be quiet on command. It is perhaps best to teach puppies how to be silent before they enter training, for a dog in protection work training is alert and excited by his environment and often reacts by barking. Best to avoid this before it becomes a habit.

First, your puppy has to understand what is expected of him, so begin in a relaxed way at home. When your dog is lying at your feet or you are sitting beside him, ask a helper to ring the doorbell or knock at the door. When your dog starts barking, say, "Quiet," or "Silent." When he stops barking, reward him with a treat or a toy to play with.

After a while, as always, your dog will learn what is expected. The next step is to go outside, again asking a helper to make a noise or strange sounds from some distance away. Stay with your dog, give him the command for silence, and reward him when he stops barking. Your attitude, and the manner in which you speak the command—somewhat excited and whispery—makes it clear to your dog what you want him to do. Again, you can combine the command with a discreet hand signal.

So far, so good! Your puppy is controlling himself, so gradually reduce the distance between him and where your helper is hiding, making strange noises. In the end, your puppy should be able to sit or lie down quietly and listen to the sounds without reacting.

If a puppy understands how to be still and quiet regardless of what is going on around him, he will be able to take on those parts of protection work that require a quiet dog: for example, when the decoy stands still.

Exercise 3: Puppy Bite Work

The first steps you take with your seven-month-old dog to prepare him for protection training involve a lot of play, and this may seem trivial. However, not only does playing with your dog cement the bond between the two of you, but playing also helps your young dog learn skills that will help him later as he trains for the IGP trials.

Fighting games between handler and dog are fantastic exercises. Their value cannot be overestimated for a future reliable Schutzhund because these games not only help your dog to understand that he must be prepared for any eventuality, but also that he must be obedient to you. Fighting games truly make a team out of you and your dog even as they give you both a great work out.

Take a puppy rag by its handle and move it back and forth in front of your dog and also pull it along the ground. Encourage your dog to catch the rag with "Go on," and keep it up until your dog catches and bites it. When your dog catches the rag, ensure that he holds it in his mouth by pulling on it as soon as he bites in. Pull with a force equal to that of your puppy's. When he feels that resistance, your dog will fight against it. If there is no resistance, he will likely drop the rag soon after biting it.

When playing this game with your puppy, only offer as much resistance as that given by your dog. Don't let your puppy know that humans are stronger! If your dog pulls the rag away from you, pull back with equal force. Draw the rag back, then pay it out again, saying "Good boy, go on" each time.

Once your puppy has hung on to the rag for about a minute, pull the rag quietly toward you over the ground. Your dog should be holding on, but not actively pulling on the rag at this point. Then, offer him a treat and praise him with "Good boy, out" when he releases the rag and takes the treat. When he has gulped the treat, hold the rag out for your puppy again so that he knows he can bite the rag again as a reward for such a good "Out." In this way, your dog learns that "Out" is rewarded not only by a treat, but also by another round of the game.

Three Important Commands

As your dog becomes more and more interested in the biting game and better at biting and releasing, you can begin to carefully introduce three important commands: "Watch him," "Go on," and "Out." The command "Watch him" prepares your dog for the coming fight, but it is not meant to encourage your dog to fight. The command to fight is "Go on." In countries, however, where it is against the law to set your dog on people, we recommend that you use another command for bite work, such as "Help" or "Defend." Really, however, the words mean nothing to the dog, so "Help" or "Defend" represent the same thing as "Go on."

A Schutzhund is expected first to defend only on command. To teach your dog this, he first must learn what "defense" is. Defense means fight, so you must teach him to fight. It is important, however, never to shape your dog into a fighting machine that is so sharp and toothy that nobody can get near him. Such dogs can never be used in the IGP program. Before a dog can learn when he must bite, he must learn when not to bite.

Exercise 4: Out

If you teach your dog the command to bite, you must also teach him the command to release, or "Out." In a Schutzhund, we want a courageous dog, but we also want a dog that immediately obeys the softest-spoken command. You can achieve this when your dog knows the three important commands "Watch him," "Go on," and "Out." At the command to be attentive ("Watch him"), your dog has to watch the decoy's movements. At the command to defend ("Go on"), your dog is allowed to bite the offered tug or sleeve. At the command to release ("Out"), your dog is under no circumstances allowed to bite, or when he is biting, he has to release immediately. If you have a sharp dog that does not respond to "Out," unpleasant things may happen. Make sure this is not the case with your dog! To teach "Out," train your puppy to play the fighting game that follows.

First, show your dog the rag in such a way that he cannot bite it. In a quiet tone, say, "Watch him," and keep the rag in front of him. Then hit the ground with the rag and encourage the dog with "Go on" to catch the rag. If your dog bites the rag, praise him with

"Good boy, go on," and then tug at the rag with a force equal to that of your dog's. After about half a minute, command your dog to "Out" briefly.

When he releases the rag, don't hold it high above your dog, but keep it on the ground within your dog's reach, and then give him the command "Go on," allowing him the opportunity to bite again as a reward for releasing. This way, the release is followed immediately by the invitation to bite again. Your dog will love this game. After the last "Out" of your training session, reward your dog again by throwing a ball or giving him a treat.

Your dog's character will dictate how you train him to bite and release. Sharp dogs, for example, need little bite training but more "Out" training. We allow sharp dogs to pull the rag or tug more briefly, but we lengthen the sequence after the "Out." In this manner, we put more emphasis on suppressing than on promotion of the bite drive. We handle dogs that are hesitant to bite differently, letting them pull the rag more often and longer, and training the "Out" less often and more briefly. When the hesitant dog's drive to bite comes to the fore, the training can follow the normal pattern used with dogs that bite easily.

Hesitant Young Dogs

You can teach your hesitant young dog to bite by playing with him. Use a soft, French-linen puppy rag or a fluffy rag, and soon enough he will bite and keep the rag in his mouth, regarding it as conquered prey. Start by swinging the rag in front of your little dog, without touching him. Most likely, your puppy will be interested in it and will try to get it. Allow this, but don't let the rag go. Your dog will try to draw the rag toward himself by working with his front legs and tugging the rag, using his mouth and neck muscles. While this is happening, play calmly with the rag and don't make any sudden movements. Don't draw your dog up high or even tug too hard in your direction. See it as a quiet game, in which you draw the rag toward you and a moment later let it go a bit. Let the rag go after a few seconds of play.

Now, watch your puppy. What he does with the rag now that he has it is very important. Does he treat it as prey and walk away with it very proudly, or does he let the rag go and lose interest in it? If your dog lets the rag go almost immediately, try to entice him with it again, moving the rag as if you want to take the prey away from him. Perhaps your little dog will like that game and will pick up the rag again and take it away. Let your dog hold it in his mouth as you tug at it briefly. Make sure that your puppy wins the game and that he can proudly walk away with the rag. When you take too long to release the rag, your dog may release it, and that is not the goal of the game. Your dog has to be victorious and take the rag away from you. Slowly increase the length of time you play the game before releasing the rag. In the meantime, observe how your dog's behavior is developing. Through these games, most hesitant dogs become interested in biting the rag and carrying it away.

Aggressive Young Dogs

If your dog becomes aggressive when you play biting games and wildly pulls on the rag, do not allow him to walk away with the rag. When your dog becomes aggressive, stop pulling on the rag and wait until he is quieter. With a friendly spoken "Out," take the rag out of his mouth. Remember not to force your dog to release the rag by pressing his lip against his teeth to open his mouth, but simply wave a treat in front of his nose and he will open his mouth. Praise your little dog with "Good boy, out" when he leaves the rag and takes the snack. Maintain a quiet demeanor and do not use violence against your young dog. Instead, make sure the game is always fun for both of you. After having to take the rag away from your dog, put it away.

Next time, use a training tug, which allows your dog to practice a proper bite.

Average Young Dogs

Your dog may also react to the biting game like any average dog (as far as such a thing exists, because every dog is unique) and play happily with the rag without becoming aggressive. As per the game described, let him walk away with the rag until he lets it go. Then carefully try to steal it away, and watch to find out if your dog becomes interested in it again. After you have done that once, at the most twice, quit. Dogs that aren't terribly interested in the rag can be stimulated by this type of play. However, playing this game once a day is more than enough because you still have a lot of time to train your puppy, and you want him to maintain an interest in biting games.

When your puppy understands the biting game, ask a friend to play with him and the rag, and later on with the tug, in your presence. Make sure your friend knows what has to happen and show him how to play the game properly: no threatening behavior allowed. It is important that you, not your friend, praise your dog while he is biting with "Good boy." After your friend lets the rag go and your dog walks away as the winner, continue praising. When your dog lets the rag fall, ask your friend to try once again, carefully, to take the rag away. Ideally your dog will not allow that and will quickly take the rag somewhere else. Make sure your friend does not try more than twice to take the rag away. After that, it is time to round off the game with much praise, as you have always done when playing this game.

Making Progress

Do not overdo things with your puppy by trying to make progress too quickly, and never force the game on your little dog when he does not feel like playing. As soon as he stops showing interest in

playing, you should quit the session. Graduate from the rag to the
tug when your dog understands the rag-bite game. Always remember that your young dog's teeth are changing and not planted very
solidly in his jaws: play carefully.

If you have been playing the bite game with your puppy for
a while—and if your dog has a sound fighting instinct—you
should be able to graduate to the tug. With the tug, you don't
have to repeat the game as often; every other day, or twice a week
is enough. However, if your dog isn't very interested in the game,
you can help him develop fighting instincts and courage, as well as
self-confidence, by playing a bit more often.

When you introduce a friend to the game, don't go much
further than asking that person to play along. Ask your friend
to hold the tug with both hands, which will help her counter-
balance your dog's actions. No one should ever twist the tug in
your dog's mouth or jerk his head during the game. Once he
has bitten into the tug, your movements (or that of your friend)
should be limited to rhythmic, light, figure-eight, and easy up-
and-down or left-to-right, movements. After a brief sequence of
these movements, whoever is playing releases the tug, or stands
still, and then you command, "Out." Remember that your dog is
always a "Very good boy" when he is biting the tug or releasing
on command.

Getting Used to the Harness

As you prepare your pup for protection training, you can also get
him used to wearing a wide leather collar for protection work or,
better, a padded agitation harness with a Y-shaped chest plate. At
first, walk with your dog as he wears the harness; after a while
the harness won't irritate or distract him anymore. We prefer an
agitation harness with a Y-shaped chest plate because this design
prevents the strangling that can happen with chest straps that can
move up to the dog's throat.

The best training harness is a padded one with a Y-shaped chest plate.

Getting Used to the Soft Stick

Another thing your young dog can learn to get used to is the presence of the soft stick, if you live in a country that allows the stick test during IGP trials. (In countries that prohibit the stick test, IGP tests are implemented without it.) If you live in a country that allows work with the soft stick, you can introduce your dog to it, but be careful as you do so. Take the soft stick with you on a walk, or when your dog is walking around in your yard. Never wave the stick or threaten your dog with it.

Begin by caressing your dog with the stick; run it over your dog's back, first with the grain then against. Some dogs like this and will stand still, relishing the attention; others try to get the stick. Do not allow your dog to bite the stick! Also, make sure you are not poking or prodding your dog, or causing pain another way. Regularly pet your dog's back with the stick, saying "Good boy."

Some exercises are too difficult for young dogs, emotionally and physically. Be aware of your puppy's limitations as you embark on protection training.

After some weeks of this, your dog will be used to the stick and you can begin to tap the stick lightly and carefully on your dog's back as you caress him. Be careful not to knock wildly or heavily. By repeating this regularly, you can gradually acquaint your dog with the idea of pressure from the stick. Make sure you don't hit your young dog with the stick. The only goal for a young dog relative to the soft stick is that he is used to it making contact with his back.

If you begin to prepare your dog for IGP training with the exercises we have described in this chapter, your young dog should be ready to begin protection work at the right time. Further training, described in the next chapters, will make your dog a reliable Schutzhund.

16

Training without a Decoy

In the last decade, much has changed in protection work training. In previous years, one provoked the dog during bite work, but today, we concentrate on training the dog's self-control through positive reinforcement. We now ensure the dog has superior obedience during Phase C, and above all we value the relationship and bond between handler and dog. All of these pieces put together during training lead to a controlled and confident dog at the IGP trials and beyond.

You will work both with and without a decoy to train your dog for the Phase C exercises. This chapter is devoted to those exercises that you alone will work on with your dog, that is, all the necessary, obedience-related exercises in Phase C: Search for the Decoy, Hold and Bark, taking the dog to the place where the Preventing an Escape by the Decoy exercise happens, and the Back and/or Side Transport exercises.

Exercise 1: Search for the Decoy

In this exercise we want to see a fast-working and active dog that responds quickly to his handler's command and runs from the middle of the field to the indicated blind, looks into it carefully and thoroughly, and goes around it tightly to return to his handler, who then sends the dog along to the next blind. Of course, by the time the dog is at an exam, he already knows that the decoy is always in the sixth blind. (To make sure your dog does not rush to the last blind, during training give your dog unexpected rewards in the other blinds.)

To build up your dog's skills in this exercise, you can use food or a prey reward. You may wish to use a small blind during training so you can easily see what your dog is doing in and around the blind. Choose the treat your dog loves best for food rewards. If your dog is really fond of playing with a ball, you may wish to make the ball a prey reward. What reward you choose all depends on your dog.

USING FOOD REWARDS

When using food rewards to train your dog to perform this exercise, set up one small blind. Stand at the closed outside top of the blind and then lead your dog around the blind, enticing him with a treat. Allow your dog to eat a bit of the treat as you circle around. When you come back to the start of your circle, step back from the blind and reward your dog again. Repeat this exercise several times, each time diminishing the amount of treat your dog consumes as you walk, but always providing a jackpot of treats at the end of the circle. After some training, try using an arm movement to ask your dog to circle the blind. As soon as your dog goes around the blind encouraged only by your arm movement, add the command for this exercise ("Search").

Try to teach your dog to round the blind correctly from the beginning. Although the IGP regulations do not describe the direction in which your dog must go around the blind, it is best to teach your dog to go from the top of the blind back toward to you. This way, your dog will round the blind tightly and attentively, will be under your control, and later on—in training as well as in trials—this manner of searching the blinds will prevent your dog from running from the fourth blind to the sixth, where the helper is hidden.

As soon as you and your dog can perform this exercise with the small blind successfully, set up a second small blind not far away from the first. This time, stand between the blinds and send your

Teach your dog to move around the small blind tightly and attentively.

When you are training your dog to investigate the blind carefully, reward him for his work. Because you will not be at the blind to give him a treat, allow your dog to help himself to his reward! Place the treat on top of a small table in the blind.

dog out to the first blind with your arm movement and command. When he successfully rounds that first blind and returns to you, give him his reward and then send him around the second blind. If everything goes well, work up to adding another two or three blinds. At first, reward your dog after every rounding; then only after every two roundings.

The next step in training is to place a little table inside each blind that can hold a treat; a cup on a pin placed in the ground works well. Never put the food reward on the ground; this only invites your dog to sniff the ground in and maybe even outside the blind. Your dog has to find his reward easily on top of the table, which should be about 12 to 16 inches (30–40 cm) above the ground.

The disadvantage of this reward system is that you need someone to put the treat on the stand, and also your dog gets a reward even if he runs to the blind before receiving your command. Consider using a remote-controlled reward dispenser, such as the Treat & Train, to avoid these problems; it will allow you to efficiently and correctly reward your dog's behavior. These dispensers can dramatically increase the speed, precision, and effectiveness of your positive-reinforcement training. Place the reward dispenser inside the blind, also on a little table about 12 to 16 inches (30–40 cm) high.

The first order of business with this exercise is to show your dog that he can expect to find a reward inside the small blinds. Bring your dog to the first blind and show him the treat on the table or in the bowl of the reward dispenser, and let him eat that treat. Move away from the blind with your dog and then send him there from a distance to gather another treat. Repeat this a few times until he knows where to find the reward.

At this point in training, you can also begin teaching your dog how to correctly go around a normal-sized blind. Stand at the closed outside part of the blind, show your dog the treat that you've placed near the blind opening, let him take the treat, and then immediately go back to the closed outside part of the blind. From there, call your dog to you and give him a treat straight away as a reward for coming. Slowly, make the distances to and from the blind greater.

USING A BALL AS A REWARD

If you decide that a prey reward (a ball) is better suited to your dog, use a remote-controlled ball machine, such as the Dogtrace d-ball machine, hung at the top of your small blind. Before this will work, however, you must show your dog how the ball dropper works. Show him how you put a tennis ball into the machine and then let it drop a ball out, so your dog can catch and play with it. Of course, you'll have to repeat this quite a few times for your dog to understand the concept of this ball machine in the blind. When he knows what the machine does, send your dog to the blind from a distance. As soon as he gets the ball, call him—"Here"—and show him another, favorite ball, which he can take after releasing the tennis ball.

As you are teaching him to retrieve the ball from the blind, try to train him to round the blind in the best way—from the top to the bottom—by sending him to the blind from a position at the topside of the blind. As soon as he is running to the blind, step backward to call your dog from the downside of the blind. Again, slowly make your dog's journey to and from the blind longer and longer.

FAST AND FUN

When you train your dog to perform the Search for the Decoy exercise without a decoy, he does not have to worry about bite work. Without the decoy, the exercise is one of obedience and is fun for your dog even as it makes him perform quickly and precisely. You reinforce the behaviors that you want to see: looking inside a blind, getting the reward, and moving tightly around the blind and back to you for the jackpot reward. Even very young dogs can be trained in this way, bite-work free.

If your dog loves to run and enjoys retrieving his reward in the small blind, you might want to use a normal-sized blind during training. As soon as he takes the food reward in the first blind, call him to you and then send him to the second blind, where he will find another treat. If you are using a ball machine as a reward and your dog emerges from the blind with the ball, command, "Out," and immediately send him on to the second blind to get another ball from a second ball machine.

When your dog is used to working with two normal blinds and getting a reward in each, you can start training him to receive no reward in the first blind. To avoid frustrating your dog with this new step in the training, work with short distances to and from the blinds and call your dog as soon as he reaches that first blind, showing him the reward you hold in your hand and then giving it to him as soon as he arrives at your side. If you are using a ball reward, allow your dog to play with it briefly and then release it. After treats or ball time, send your dog on to the second blind, where he will get his usual reward.

Exercise 2: Hold and Bark

This exercise, too, can be trained without the help of a decoy. Here, we want the dog to actively and attentively hold the decoy and bark continuously. First, teach your dog to hold and bark for rewards at home—for example, barking for the food bowl before eating. Approach your dog with his food bowl in hand, and when you are close, command him to begin barking. Your dog should bark until you ask him to be silent. As soon as he stops barking, give your dog his food bowl. This exercise is helpful for both the Hold and Bark exercise and for the silence necessary when you call your dog from the Hold and Bark position into the heeling position.

You may choose to use a ball instead of food as the reward in teaching your dog the Hold and Bark. If so, when training, hold the ball high above his nose, and then command your dog to bark. Let him bark for about 20 seconds, and then command him to be silent. As soon as he stops barking, give him the ball as a reward.

Because dogs learn very quickly from concept training when it is done correctly, all the pieces of the exercise should always be trained in the same way. So, it's important that you always take up the same conspicuous position when training the Hold and Bark with the food bowl or the ball. Stand upright as you would during a trial, facing forward and not looking at your dog.

IN AND OUT OF THE BLIND

Begin training the Hold and Bark in the blind by first hanging a remote-controlled ball machine at the top of the blind. If

A remote-controlled ball machine hung at the top of the blind helps in training the Hold and Bark exercise.

you would rather use food rewards, place the remote-controlled reward dispenser in the blind at a height of about 12 to 16 inches (30–40 cm) from the ground.

When everything is set up, send your dog to the blind with the command "Search." When he gets there and expects to get a ball, wait until he begins to bark, or give the command "Bark." After he barks for about 20 seconds, press the button that dispenses the ball or the treat. In later training sessions, your dog must first bark and then be silent on command before he can receive his reward.

Train your dog to bark on command before training him to be silent. Move to your barking dog at the blind, which should be in the basic position. For silence, command, "Heel." He should take up the position silently and sit correctly in the basic position until you command, "Free," "Yes," or "Okay," at which point your dog is allowed to have the ball or treat from the machine.

After the above is done correctly, place yourself two paces back from your sitting dog and call him to heel in the basic position.

Don't give your dog a ball or treat from the machine at this point, but do give him the same sort of ball or treat he would receive from the machine. From two paces away, slowly progress to positioning yourself about five paces away, which is the distance stipulated for this exercise by the IGP regulations.

Exercise 3: Preventing an Escape by the Decoy

During this exercise, the decoy moves from the blind at a normal pace to the location designated for his "escape." At the direction of the judge, take your free-heeling dog to a marked spot, where your dog should lie down before the escape happens. Your dog has to heel happily, quickly, and attentively, aligned with your knee. Prior to the command "Down," your dog should sit in the basic position, straight, calmly, and attentively. He has to directly and quickly follow the "Down" command and remain lying down in the designated location calmly and confidently, all the while paying close attention to the decoy.

Because this is an obedience exercise, you can teach it to your dog without the help of a decoy. For this exercise, make sure there is something attractive in the vicinity that your dog can attend to. Here, again, you can use the remote-controlled reward (ball or treat) machine, which you place about five paces from the spot where you bring the dog into the Down position. A ball launcher, such as a Smartfetch Up ballshooter, works well if you are working with a ball—if you place the launcher at a slant, the ball will travel over almost the same distance that a decoy will travel as he tries to escape.

Another, cheaper method is to place a ball bigger than a tennis ball, one that your dog loves to play with, somewhere he can see it, and train him to heel from the blind to the spot where he has to lie down. Then, step back to the blind. When you are sure that your dog is focused on the ball, give the command "Go on," and he will get up quickly and take his beloved ball. Eventually, just before the command, someone can kick the ball away, thus introducing motion to the exercise.

A remote-controlled ball launcher can help you train your dog to master the Preventing an Escape by the Decoy exercise. Place the ball launcher about five paces from the spot where you ask your dog to lie down.

Transport

According to the IGP testing regulations, the Side Transport of the decoy takes place over a distance of about 20 paces and the command to "Heel," or the preferable "Transport," is permitted. Your dog is to walk along at the right side of the decoy, so that he is between you and the decoy. During the transport, your dog has to pay close attention to the decoy. He may not, however, crowd the decoy, jump on him, or grip. The group stops in front of the judge.

In the IGP 2 and 3 tests there is also a Back Transport exercise over a distance of approximately 30 normal paces. For this exercise, you should use the command "Transport." The judge determines how you and your dog will conduct the Back Transport. However, in general, you order the decoy to move out, with your off-leash dog, which is closely watching the decoy, following approximately five paces behind. This distance of five paces must be maintained throughout the Back Transport.

Exercise 5: Back Transport

Back Transport is also an obedience exercise that your dog can learn at home or elsewhere, using either a big ball your dog loves to play with, or a remote-controlled ball launcher. Place the ball or launcher about 10 paces in front of your sitting dog. Ask him to take the basic position with the command "Heel"; at this point, your dog should be looking at your face. Then give the command "Transport" while looking at the ball or launcher, and as soon as your dog looks at the ball or launcher, command him to "Go on," which is the cue for him to take the ball and play with it briefly. Practice this exercise in different locations.

When practicing the Back Transport exercise, use a big ball as a reward. Ask your dog to assume the basic position with "Heel." Your dog should look at your face when he is in that position.

When you are sure the dog is attentive and in the correct basic position, speak the command "Transport." Turn your attention to the big ball, and as soon as your dog also shifts his gaze to the ball, tell him to "Go on," which is his cue to take the ball and play with it.

A helper with a ball can take the place of the big ball in this exercise. If your dog is walking correctly during the Back Transport, you should be able to feel his body brush up against your leg. You shouldn't have to look down to monitor your dog's form—you should be able to feel it!

As you progress in training, you can add more distance to the Back Transport, making left and right turns, before allowing your dog to take the ball as a reward.

When your dog understands this part of the exercise, after the command "Transport," walk forward two or three paces, keeping your dog close to your leg, heeling to your knee. When you are walking this close together, you don't have to look down to see if your dog is walking correctly because you can feel his movements. Make sure your dog does not go in front. If he does well, give your dog the command to "Go on" to get the ball. When your dog understands this exercise, try taking more paces and make right and left turns before you allow him to take the ball.

Exercise 8: Side Transport

When you train the Side Transport exercise, you will need a helper but not necessarily a decoy. Anyone who can hold a ball will fit the bill. Ask your helper to stand and hold a ball in front of his body. Call your dog into the basic position with "Heel"—again, your dog should be looking at your face. Then, walk with your heeling dog to the right side of the helper and give the command "Transport." Your dog is now allowed to look at the ball, but he has stay with you, in contact with your leg.

Again, try doing this over the course of two or three paces, and at your command to "Go on," the helper throws the ball and your dog is allowed to fetch it and play. If everything is going well, try extending the distance you walk toward the helper and ball, and curve to the left and right—don't make right-angle turns—while walking. As well, you can add another helper and the soft stick into the mix. In this version of the exercise, your ball-holding helper should hold the soft stick, as well. When you reach him,

While you practice the Side Transport exercise, your dog is allowed to look at the ball in front of the helper's body, but his body must maintain contact with your leg.

take the soft stick away and step away with "Heel," not allowing your dog to take the ball from the helper. Transport the first helper to the second helper. Stop in front of the second helper and give him the soft stick you took from the first helper. At this point, reward your dog by throwing a different ball.

The Decoy

If your dog has mastered all of the above exercises, you need a decoy to help you train your dog to bite. But before embarking on serious bite work, you need 100 per cent control over your dog, and your dog has to be physically and mentally mature. After your dog teethes (at about seven or eight months), see how he does when biting a rag or tug. If he isn't interested, try to encourage his prey drive, as is suggested in the previous chapter. If your dog is biting well, try the preliminary exercises suggested in this chapter and wait to begin bite work until your dog is 13 or 14 months old, depending on his level of maturity.

A good decoy is invaluable to your dog's training in protection work. His tasks are to:

- Encourage the prey drive in your dog, if necessary, through prey games with the rag or tug that might be bound to a rod to allow your dog to chase the "prey." For lively dogs, such as Malinois, this will not be necessary and may even cause trouble, making the dog lose control. However, other dogs, such as Rottweilers or Bouvier des Flandres, may require this kind of encouragement.

- Improve your dog's grip. A full bite is necessary because the strongest grip is the one that includes the dog's molars.

- Train the Separation phase, wherein your dog transitions from having a good grip to releasing his grip on the command "Out." Here a change in drive has to take place: from powerful bite work, the dog has to shift into obedience. Remember here that a fast "Out" on your dog's part should always result in a "Good boy" from you! As well, you should almost immediately command your dog to bite again to reward him for releasing quickly and obediently.

- Train the Guarding phase, wherein your dog must be silent, watching the decoy's every move. The decoy looks at the dog to gauge if he is attentive and exuding pressure as he guards. As a reward for intense guarding, the decoy may attack your dog by first moving the soft stick and the sleeve, and later on only the soft stick. In this case, your dog is allowed to react by biting the sleeve.

- Train the Pressure phase by means of his dynamic moves. Once your dog grips well, the decoy will begin pressure work with the soft stick. In training, your dog is allowed to take the sleeve with him after the decoy administers the touches with the soft stick. In the Pressure phase, your dog needs to bite quietly without re-biting. The decoy knows that this phase needs to be built up step by step, without too much pressure applied all at once.

17

Building Up Protection Work

Dogs in the IGP program are mostly trained using the prey-drive method. You teach your dog that he will always come out of the fight as the victor, and in training he is allowed to keep the tug or sleeve for a while and parade around with it, showing all and sundry his prize.

In the prey-drive method, young dogs first are trained with a prey-drive training rag or a big tug with two handles. One of the decoy's most tiring tasks is working with a dog and a rag or tug; this kind of work demands much physical power and energy. First, however, you, the handler, must make it clear to your young and inexperienced dog what behaviors are expected. Youngsters are always pepped up by the acts of the decoy in the thick of a fight, and most of the time they are not obedient enough to train with him.

After the decoy lets your dog win the fight and take the sleeve, his arms and upper body are relatively unprotected. For this reason, when your dog first begins training, he should do so on a leash. If you can't control your dog—maybe you distract him while he is training—the instructor will handle him using a long line. Remember that while training with the decoy, your dog should always wear a wide leather collar or a padded agitation harness with a Y-shaped chest plate (not a harness with a chest strap, which can strangle your dog if it rides up to his throat during exercises).

Working with the Tug

When you train with the tug, start by standing with your on-leash dog on the training field as the decoy (wearing all of his protection clothes and carrying the tug or rag) approaches in a quiet and nonthreatening way. When he is about 16 feet (5 m) in front of you, he stops, silent. Only when your dog reacts—by barking, for example—will the decoy spring into action.

After your dog reacts to the decoy, he approaches him in a sidelong fashion, starts teasing him with the rag or tug, and displays hitting movements in the dog's direction. As soon as your dog lunges at the decoy, the latter reacts by submissively running away, which, of course, increases your dog's prey drive. If your dog has reacted to the decoy correctly, continue on to the next step in the following session.

The next time, the decoy approaches your dog, moving the tug around a lot; keep your dog on a short leash and stay close to him, giving him the support he needs in the face of this bad guy! When the decoy is a few yards away from your dog—and depending on your dog's response—he will flee and then once again approach your dog in a hunched, fearful pose.

During this exercise, make sure you don't jerk at your dog's leash, but maintain supple tension on the line. Meanwhile, the decoy has to make sure he doesn't hit the dog's legs, body, or head when he moves the tug up and down in front of your dog in a nonthreatening way. He holds the tug with two hands, one on either end, freeing up the middle for the dog to bite. When your dog has gripped the tug, the decoy makes smooth figure eight motions with it, and your dog will offer resistance. The decoy allows the dog to grip for a short time, and then he lets your dog win by letting go of the tug at the right moment, which is when the dog tugs. The dog will feel that he has overcome the decoy, and the decoy fearfully backs away from the dog. After the fight, you, the handler, should praise your dog and accompany him as he proudly carries the tug around and off the field.

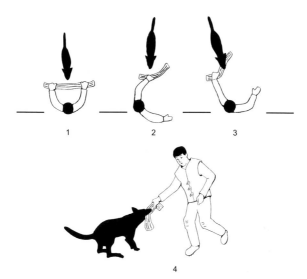

Illustrations 1 through 3 demonstrate how a young dog can bite into a rolled up rag or a tug. The decoy always stays the same distance away from the dog to minimize the threat. Illustration 4 shows the side view of illustration 3. The dog should be on leash in every one of these positions.

In illustrations 1 and 4, the dog guards the decoy. In illustration 2, the decoy attacks the dog by taking a step forward to the left or right. In illustrations 3 and 5, the dog has bitten into the tug, and the decoy begins fighting. The handler has his dog on leash throughout the exercise.

If your dog understands and likes this game, the decoy will allow the fight to go on longer and involve more energetic moves in coming sessions, but it will remain a nonthreatening game until the time comes when you no longer allow your dog to parade around the field with the tug/prize. In this scenario, your dog wins the tug as usual and releases it on his own, or on command, but the exercise ends with the decoy taking the tug and fleeing in fear. When the decoy takes the tug, make sure your dog stays attentive to the tug but does not make a move to take it.

Threatening with the Hand

When your dog has increased confidence as a result of the above game, a change in training tactics occurs. From this step forward in the training, three exercises can be brought into play: the Guarding, the Escape, and the Attack On the Dog. As always, the decoy approaches your dog when he is concentrating on the actively moving burlap tug. During the fight that ensues, the decoy is actively in motion but not too predictable or repetitive, and he eggs your dog on with this active behavior. The decoy should not work roughly and should always be attentive to your dog's reactions and behavior.

If all is going well, the exercise continues as always, but the decoy tries to add something threatening into the mix. The decoy holds the tug in his left hand (for a right-handed decoy, or in his right hand for a left-handed decoy) as the dog bites; he must be very close to the dog at this point. If he is close enough, the decoy pulls the dog a bit closer still and then threatens your dog with his free arm. He swings his arm all the way down, then up high above your dog. As he does this, the decoy watches to see if your dog closes his eyes or otherwise yields to the threat. If this happens, the decoy knows he must step back in the training and give your dog more time to build self-confidence before trying that move again.

In illustrations 1 and 2, the decoy lets the dog tug the rag too far away and therefore cannot threaten effectively. Illustrations 3 and 4 show the decoy in a better position. Again, the dog is on leash in all positions.

If your dog doesn't show fear, you can continue on with the training, and the decoy can go on threatening by touching your dog on the spot he will later touch with the soft stick. As soon as the decoy touches him with the flat of his hand, he praises your dog with "Good boy," and a bit later your dog wins the fight. At this level, the decoy doesn't threaten your dog with his voice; on the contrary, the decoy encourages your dog. As soon as your dog is biting well and with increasing ferocity, the decoy will start to build up the physically threatening part of the exercise, and after that he introduces spoken threats.

Ten Points of Attention for Handlers and Decoys

1. Always work calmly, and do not let the dog bark when he comes to the training field for protection work.

2. The dog has to be quiet, especially when he is learning protection exercises. Prevent the dog from switching into a high drive; remember that dogs learn best in a lower drive.

3. When training with the tug, give the dog the chance to bite in very well; do not push the tug too deeply into his mouth, but let him grip the tug on his own. The decoy can help by working steadily and giving the dog every opportunity to bite correctly.

4. During the fight, the decoy should stay focused on the dog and not work too wildly. Instead he should move actively and energetically but in a controlled way.

5. If you hold the tug with both hands, make sure you are holding the ends of the tug, leaving the middle part open to the dog, otherwise the dog could bite you.

6. If the dog has bitten in, do not push the ends of the tug together, because this will bind the dog's muzzle.

7. Take care to use a good-quality tug. Always use a burlap tug, not one made of plastic or nylon because these cut into the dog's gums.

8. As you work, watch that the dog is not getting too tired; a tired dog feels weak and becomes unsure. Always end the bite work when the dog is at his strongest and can leave the field as a victor.

9. Repeat training exercises with the burlap tug over the course of many weeks so the dog becomes confident in his abilities and begins to bite fully and with conviction. When this is the case, you can start to teach the dog to "Out" on command, and also to bite the puppy sleeve.

10. When the dog correctly bites the puppy sleeve, you can graduate to a normal, hard sleeve and begin teaching the exercise Search for the Decoy.

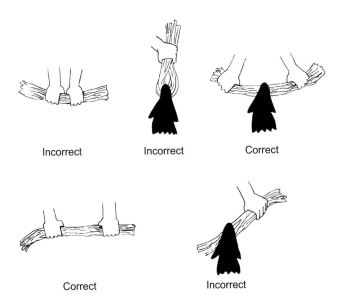

| Incorrect | Incorrect | Correct |

| Correct | Incorrect |

Correct and incorrect ways to hold the rolled rag or burlap tug at this stage of training.

The Puppy Sleeve

Dogs that have worked longer with the tug often begin their first sleeve work with a soft sleeve called a puppy sleeve. The dog's first bite on the puppy sleeve is important; it has to be a correct bite. Your dog has to bite fully, which means that he must bite with his mouth fully around the sleeve. Getting your dog to do that is part of the decoy's job.

As soon as your dog has bitten, a silent fight occurs; you let out your dog's leash but only so much that you are still in control. Your goals with the leash are twofold: to keep the dog from getting too close to the decoy, and to help the decoy control your dog's grip on the sleeve. The decoy does this by pulling or pushing the dog as necessary.

Another of your jobs as handler is to "fight" actively with your dog, encouraging him with "Hold it, good boy," and always keeping the leash at the same length. Never jerk on the leash, but gradually

Always finish off bite work practice with your dog feeling that he is the winner.

increase the tautness of the leash. The decoy has to be able to pull back on the sleeve a little bit and then unbend it sometimes to ensure your dog gets the best grip. He must, without being wild, move well and never turn the sleeve so that your dog bites into it at an angle. In bite work, the decoy's timing is crucial to your dog's success. When he is ready to allow your dog to take the sleeve and win the fight, the decoy waits until your dog is standing with all four legs on the ground. If he lets go when the sleeve is up, your dog could fall.

Normally, the fight ends when you command, "Out," or when the decoy releases the sleeve. If your dog proudly walks around with the sleeve/prey and does not intend to release it, take your dog to your car or his crate or kennel. When you get there, praise him thoroughly and quietly take the sleeve away from him. Ask him to "Out," and if that doesn't work, exchange the sleeve for some treats. Always praise and reward your dog for the good work, even if he is reluctant to give up the sleeve.

More Threatening

When your dog has reacted well a few times to the threatening arm, the decoy can adjust his posture so he is standing more upright and then approach the dog in a slightly more threatening manner. He should not ever overdo it, nor stand upright and

1   2

In illustration 1, the decoy touches the dog where he will later apply pressure with the soft stick. Illustration 2 shows the decoy snatching the rag or tug after the dog has dropped it.

threaten all at once; as with all the training we have described in this book, the step-by-step approach that quietly increases difficulty is best. If your dog ever becomes insecure, take a step back in training by presenting a less-threatening decoy. Even for dogs that are reacting well, you must not offer too much of a threat all at once. At this stage, especially, a lot of dogs are ruined because the handler wants to make progress too quickly.

At this point, we have reached the phase where the dog is experiencing the full threat of the decoy and is biting directly and fully. Even so, now is not the time to start introducing pressure with the soft stick. Eventually, you can carefully threaten stronger dogs with the soft stick, but wait until your dog is really strong before actually touching him with it; in the heat of the fight, he will hardly feel a light touch with the soft stick.

Stronger and Stronger

When your dog is biting well, you and the decoy can start teaching him to chase and bite a decoy who is running away. To do this, the decoy walks threateningly toward your dog and then turns when he is about a yard away from him, walking back to where he came from at a brisk pace. Immediately after this, let your dog off the leash, and he may bite the decoy. A good decoy is able to catch your dog properly when he lunges to bite, keeping the sleeve to the side of his body and giving your dog every chance to bite well. If this is successful, the decoy will slowly increase the distance he walks away from your dog. Following this, the decoy will only try the next step—walking back toward your dog in a threatening way after the flight—if he feels your dog is really strong enough for it. Again, begin carefully and quietly and introduce every piece of the exercise to your dog step by step.

The whole protection program is, just like all other phases of IGP, focused on making the dog's self-confidence stronger. This means that you, the handler, must also have the necessary self-confidence so you can pass it along to your dog. The handler always has to keep the big picture in mind to be able to handle and support his dog correctly. A part of supporting your dog correctly is knowing when to talk to the instructor and decoy about training procedures and when to remain silent.

Before every training session, the instructor tells you what is going to happen and explains what is expected of you and your dog. During some training sessions, you, the instructor, or the decoy may think that something should be done differently than what was originally planned. It is best not to discuss changes of plan on the field, but stop the exercise at the right moment, loudly praising your dog, and let the decoy disappear into a blind. Make sure you do not talk about disagreements or changes of plan while the decoy and your dog are present, because then you are not paying attention to your dog anymore, and you will perhaps forget to praise him for his good work, or even make big mistakes without knowing it. If, for example, while you are talking and the decoy moves and your dog reacts by barking, you may command your dog to be silent, instead of praising him for barking. You do not want to make such mistakes! You, as the leader of your dog's pack, have to show self-confidence during protection training and must know exactly what is going to happen. Only then can you convey self-confidence to your dog.

Hold and Bark

Start practicing the Hold and Bark exercise when your dog has already learned to bark loudly on command and his bite is sound. Stand about 11 yards (10 m) from the blind, making sure your dog can't see the decoy inside. Keep your dog on the long leash. On a signal from your instructor, the decoy starts yelling and comes out of the blind, walks around the blind, and disappears into it again. He then stands in the blind with his sleeved arm held at a slight angle, motionless, and in a nonthreatening stance. He holds a bite pillow in his armpit. As soon as the decoy disappears into the blind, send your dog over there with the command "Search." When your dog arrives at the blind and is in front of the decoy, he should start barking without prompting from you. After a while, the decoy throws the bite pillow out of the blind, which your dog is allowed to fetch and run away with as a reward. If your dog comes back to you and releases the pillow, give a command to the decoy to approach you and your dog. When you then command the decoy to take the pillow, your dog must allow him to pick it up and quietly walk back to the blind. This is the end of the exercise, so, as always, praise your dog. Repeat this exercise a few times in each training session, but not too often.

By training this exercise every time in the same way, your dog will quickly learn what he is supposed to do. The biggest mistake you can make at this point in training would be to change the way you train this exercise without giving your dog the chance to understand what is expected, thereby confusing your dog. However, if your dog's performance of this exercise is consistently sound, you can change things up a bit by having the decoy use a different blind.

After your dog has barked for a while at the decoy when practicing the Hold and Bark exercise, the decoy will reward him by throwing the bite pillow away from the blind. Your dog is then allowed to fetch the pillow and run away with it.

The next step is to end the exercise practice by standing beside your barking dog in front of the decoy in the blind and asking him to heel. Then, turn directly to the left in front of the decoy, so that you are walking between the decoy and your dog. Prevent your dog from biting and show you have control by ensuring that he heels correctly. Combining obedience training with bite work is important though often neglected, leading dogs to slip into sloppy behavior.

As you build up your dog's comfort with the Hold and Bark exercise, you are teaching him that he must bark and then guard at the blind. Never allow him to bite while guarding, otherwise there is a greater chance that he will bite instead of bark, and if the decoy does not respond, your dog may release and then bite again. When a dog behaves this way at an exam, we say that he is "eating his points," losing points for bad behavior. So, during training, the decoy must never offer the sleeve in the blind but only throw the bite pillow, and your dog must learn the Hold and Bark as an obedience exercise. Keep your dog on leash when you train this exercise until you are sure he knows it inside and out.

The Escaping Decoy

From the obedience training in Phase C, it shouldn't be a problem to progress to commanding the decoy to leave the blind and prepare for the next exercise by walking to the designated area. As you begin training the Preventing an Escape by the Decoy exercise, stay beside your dog, but as he becomes successful, walk back to the blind.

As you teach your dog this exercise, the decoy should help by keeping his sleeved arm poised and ready to catch your dog as he runs. In the first sessions the decoy makes it easy for your dog by offering the sleeve low to the ground, but he should not do that very often. Your dog has to learn that he must make the necessary effort to bite. Also, the decoy should always walk on as your dog bites. He shouldn't turn back toward the pursuing dog, not until your dog is really strong in bite work.

If training for Preventing the Escape by the Decoy is going well, the decoy can take the next step and turn on your dog to begin training for the Attack On the Dog in Motion exercise. When he is about 11 yards (10 m) ahead of your dog, the decoy should turn toward him and allow him to bite the sleeve. During this exercise, hold your dog on a long leash. When this part of the training is going well, eliminate the long leash so that your dog can freely practice the exercise. As well, slowly enlarge the distance between where your dog is to where the decoy turns to allow him to bite the sleeve, from 11 yards to 32 or 44 yards (30 or 40 m). As always, as your dog begins to know the exercise backward and forward, vary the way in which you practice it. For example, after one pursuit, let your dog guard in the expectation of a flight, and then another time work through a side

In training Attack On the Dog in Motion, the decoy "catches" your dog as he runs.

transport after a pursuit. Variety in training helps keep your dog attentive!

Guarding and Transport

As soon as your dog has prevented the decoy's escape and the fight is over, your dog must guard the decoy until released. If he releases his bite on command, observe him closely. If he stands and keeps an attentive eye on the decoy, do not pressure him to sit. If he sits or lies down without a command and pays constant attention to the decoy, that is also correct. However, if your dog walks back to you or walks around the field sniffing and loses interest in the decoy, he is missing the point of the exercise. Guarding means giving the decoy no chance to flee; your dog should not even look briefly over his shoulder to check in with you.

For the Side Transport to the Judge exercise, call your dog to the heel and walk on the right side of the decoy; on your command, "Transport," all three of you move forward. During the escort, your dog has to be focused on the decoy, but he may not bite or obstruct him. When you reach your instructor, stop and

During the Side Transport exercise, your dog must focus on
the decoy, but he may not bite or obstruct him.

hand him the soft stick. Continue to keep an eye on your dog.
He has to stay sitting during the short pause that follows the stick
hand-off. After that, you may leave the training field with your
dog. Don't forget to thank the decoy and the instructor for all their
work and help!

Bibliography

Army Headquarters. 1977. *Military police working dogs*. Washington, DC: Field Manual.

Balabanov, I., and K. Duet. 1999. *Advanced schutzhund*. New York: Howell Book House.

Barwig, S., and S. Hilliard. 1991. *Schutzhund: Theory and training methods*. New York: Howell Bookhouse.

Böttger, P. 1937. *Hunde im Dienste der Kriminalpolizei*. Zeitschrift für Hundeforschung.

Eden, R.S. 1999. *Dog training for law enforcement*. Calgary, AB: Detselig Enterprises.

Ensminger, J.J. 2012. *Police and military dogs, criminal detection, forensic evidence, and judicial admissibility*. Boca Raton, FL: CRC Press.

Fédération Cynologique Internationale. 2012. *Guidelines for the international utility dog trials and the international tracking dog trial of the FCI*. Belgium: Thuin.

Geairain, S.A. 1976. *Le pistage*. Paris: Editions Crèpin-Leblond.

Haak, R. 1984. *Het africhten tot Verdedigingshond*. Zuid Boekprodukties. Best.

Johnson, G. 1975. *Tracking dog: Theory and methods*. Rome, NY: Arner Publications.

Lancet, D. 1986. Vertebrate olfactory reception. *Annual Review of Neuroscience*, 9, 329–355.

Mackenzie, S.A. 1996. *Decoys and aggression: A police K9 training manual*. Calgary, AB: Detselig Enterprises.

———. 2009. *Aggression control: Teaching the out*. Calgary, AB: Detselig Enterprises.

Menzel, R., and R. Menzel. 1930. *Die Verwertung der Riechfähigkeit des Hundes im Dienste der Menschheit*. Linz.

Mori, K., and Y. Yoshihara. 1995. Molecular recognition and olfactory processing in the mammalian olfactory system. *Progress in Neurobiology*, 45(6), 585–619. http://dx.doi.org/10.1016/0301-0082(94)00058-P.

Most, K. 1977. *Training dogs: A manual*. London: Popular Dogs.

Raiser, H. 1981. *Der schutzhund.* Hamberg: Paul Parey Verlag.

Schoon, A. *The performance of dogs in identifying humans by scent.* PhD diss., Leiden, 1997.

Stark, C. 1998. *A dog is not a gun: Observations on canine policing.* Calgary, AB: Detselig Enterprises.

Stoddart, D.M. 1980. *The ecology of vertebrate olfaction.* London: Chapman and Hall. http://dx.doi.org/10.1007/978-94-009-5869-2.

Syrotuck, W.G. 1972. *Scent and the scenting dog. Westmoreland.* Rome, NY: Arner Publications.

Thesen, A., Steen, J.B., and Døving, K.B. 1993. Behaviour of dogs during olfactory tracking. *Journal of Experimental Biology, 180*, 247–251.

U.S. Department of Defense. 2013. *U.S. military working dog training handbook.* Guilford, CT: Lyons Press.

Yin, S., Fernandez, E.J., Pagan, S., Richardson, S.L., and Snyder, G. 2008. Efficiency of a remote-controlled, positive-reinforcement, dog-training system for modifying problem behaviors exhibited when people arrive at the door. *Applied Animal Behaviour Science, 113*, 123–138.

———. 2010. *How to behave so your dog behaves.* Neptune City, NJ: TFH Publications Inc.

About the Authors

Ruud Haak is the author of more than 30 dog books in Dutch and German. Since 1979 he has been the editor-in-chief of the biggest Dutch dog magazine, *Onze Hond (Our Dog)*. He was born in 1947 in Amsterdam, the Netherlands. At the age of 13, he was training police dogs at his uncle's security dog training center, and when

Ruud Haak and his Malinois Google van het Eldenseveld.

he was 15, he worked after school with his patrol dog (which he trained himself) at the Amsterdam harbor. He later started training his dogs in Schutzhund and IGP, and he successfully bred and showed German shepherds and Saint Bernards.

Ruud worked as a social therapist in a government clinic for criminal psychopaths. From his studies in psychology, he became interested in dog behavior and training methods for nose work, especially the tracking dog (Fährtenhund) and the search-and-rescue dog. More recently he has trained drug and explosive detector dogs for the Dutch police and the Royal Dutch Airforce. He is also a visiting lecturer at Dutch, German, and Austrian police dog schools.

In the 1970s, Ruud and his wife, **Dr. Resi Gerritsen**, a psychologist and jurist, attended many courses and symposia with their German shepherds for Schutzhund, tracking dog, and search-and-rescue dog training in Switzerland, Germany, and Austria.

Resi Gerritsen and her young Malinois
Pepper van de Denarius.

The authors would like to thank Markus, Lydia, and Patrick Mohr from Austria, and their very successful Malinois Blade von gelben Jewel, for their support in writing this book.

In 1979 they started the Dutch Rescue Dog Organization in the Netherlands. With that unit, they attended many operations responding to earthquakes, gas explosions, and, of course, lost persons in large wooded or wilderness areas. In 1990 Ruud and Resi moved to Austria, where they were asked by the Austrian Red Cross to select and train operational rescue and avalanche dogs. They lived for three years at a height of 6,000 feet (1800 m) in the Alps and worked with their dogs in search missions after avalanches.

With their Austrian colleagues, Ruud and Resi developed a new method for training search-and-rescue dogs. This way of training showed the best results after a major earthquake in Armenia (1988), an earthquake in Japan (1995), two major earthquakes in Turkey (1999), and the big earthquakes in Algeria and Iran (2003). Ruud and Resi have also demonstrated the success of their unique training methods for tracking dogs as well as search-and-rescue

dogs at the Austrian, Czech, Hungarian, and World Champion-
ships, where both were several times the leading champions.
Resi and Ruud have held many symposia and master classes
all over the world on their unique training methods, which are
featured in their books:

- *K9 Complete Care: A Manual for Physically and Mentally Healthy
  Working Dogs*
- *K9 Drug Detection: A Manual for Training and Operations*
- *K9 Explosive and Mine Detection: A Manual for Training and
  Operations*
- *The German Shepherd Dog: A Historical View of the Breed's
  Development, Prime, and Deterioration*
- *K9 Investigation Errors: A Manual for Avoiding Mistakes*
- *The Labrador Retriever: Historical Development and Use in Police,
  SAR, Hunting, Guide, and Service Work*
- *The Malinois: The History and Development of the Breed in
  Schutzhund, Detection and Police Work*
- *K9 Personal Protection: A Manual for Training Reliable Protection Dogs*
- *K9 Professional Tracking: A Complete Manual for Theory and Training*
- *K9 Scent Training: A Manual for Training Your Identification,
  Tracking and Detection Dog*
- *K9 Search and Rescue: A Manual for Training the Natural Way*
- *K9 Working Breeds: Characteristics and Capabilities*

With Simon Prins they wrote: *K9 Behavior Basics: A Manual
for Proven Success in Operational Service Dog Training*; and with
Dr. Adee Schoon, Ruud wrote *K9 Suspect Discrimination: Training and Practicing Scent Identification Line-Ups*. All of these books
were published by Detselig Enterprises Ltd., Calgary, Canada
(now Brush Education Inc.).

Ruud and Resi now live in the Netherlands. They are international judges for the International Rescue Dog Organisation
(IRO) and the Fédération Cynologique Internationale (FCI).

At the moment, Ruud and Resi are still successfully training
their dogs. You can contact the authors by email at resigerritsen@
gmail.com.